Teaching English as
a Second Language

Teaching English as a Second Language

Giving New Learners an Everyday Grammar

Richard McGarry

McFarland & Company, Inc., Publishers
Jefferson, North Carolina, and London

LIBRARY OF CONGRESS CATALOGUING-IN-PUBLICATION DATA

McGarry, Richard, 1953–
    Teaching English as a second language : giving new learners an everyday grammar / Richard McGarry.
       p.   cm.
    Includes bibliographical references and index.

ISBN 978-0-7864-7062-4
softcover : acid free paper ∞

    1. English language — Study and teaching — Foreign speakers. 2. English language — Grammar. I. Title.
PE1128.A2M386 2012
428.0071—dc23   2012021412

BRITISH LIBRARY CATALOGUING DATA ARE AVAILABLE

© 2012 Richard McGarry. All rights reserved

No part of this book may be reproduced or transmitted in any form or by any means, electronic or mechanical, including photocopying or recording, or by any information storage and retrieval system, without permission in writing from the publisher.

Front cover images © 2012 Shutterstock

Manufactured in the United States of America

McFarland & Company, Inc., Publishers
   Box 611, Jefferson, North Carolina 28640
     www.mcfarlandpub.com

This book is dedicated with love
to Carter Hammett-McGarry

Table of Contents

Acknowledgments — viii
Preface — 1
Introduction — 5

1. The Mascagni Effect — 9
2. Articles: Julie and the French Sailor — 49
3. Prepositions: It's Above Smitty's! — 64
4. The Subjunctive: If I Were a Rich Man — 82
5. Gerunds and Infinitives: Remembering Loving Camping — 91
6. Verbs: Come Together — 107
7. Negatives, Interrogatives and Imperatives: Don't Ask and Don't Tell (Manipulative Speech Acts) — 109
8. Passives: Getting Yourself Invited to Izabela's Party — 124
9. Modals: Meeting Kelly by the Tree — 130
10. Temporal Expressions: Come by, Say, the First of the Month — 139
11. Reciprocals: Backscratching — 148

Conclusion: The Zen of Grammar — 155
Appendix A: Glossary — 161
Appendix B: Internet Resources — 167
Notes — 171
Annotated Bibliography — 173
Index — 177

Acknowledgments

I would like to acknowledge the valuable contributions of the following people:

An overwhelming debt of gratitude goes to my wife Carter, who is a fine linguist in her own right. I am supremely grateful for her patience, her valuable insights and her suggestions when I hadn't the slightest idea how to proceed.

This text would have never been possible without the students in the English for Internationals class both present and past who have been patient with my ramblings and receptive to the morsels, however meager, I have tossed their way. I am often impressed by their insightful comments and their timely questions. Truly, they have enabled me to see the world and language as complex phenomena. But most importantly, they have enabled me "to see out" when I have become mired in the "hollers" of my own narrowness.

I also want to thank the students in my Structure of Modern English class now and in the past who have patiently tolerated my sometimes obscure questions and equally confusing explanations about the state of common-usage English grammar. I am very grateful for their valuable feedback in the development of this text, and for their constant skepticism of my theories, a skepticism that kept me searching for answers to my own questions of why.

A sincere, from the bottom of my heart, thank you goes to my good friend and colleague, Dr. William Wilson, musician and ESL teacher *par excellence*, who one fateful day in the fall of 2004, happened to be teaching the Intermezzo to *Cavalleria Rusticana* by Mascagni and helped coin and elucidate the Mascagni Effect, and who waded through this text with patience and good ideas.

I am grateful to my colleagues in the Department of Physiology and Neuroscience at the Medical University of South Carolina for their insights and suggestions on the neuroscience sections of this text.

Finally, the Hubbard Center for Faculty Support and Development at Appalachian State University for their financial and editorial support. Specifically, I would like to thank Ms. Kathy Isaacs, who was a supportive voice throughout the entire process. And I would be remiss if I did not extend my most heartfelt *merci* to my students at the Université d'Angers in France. They are most marvelous students and even better teachers.

Preface

Few days go by in my working life as a professor of English for international students when one or more (usually more) of my students asks me why certain things are the way they are in the grammar of English. My first inclination upon getting a real mind-bender of a question that I have no clue how to answer is to shrug in all sincerity and say, "Beats me!" or "Well! That's just the way the language works," or "It sounds better that way." Sometimes I get the urge to explain my non-answer by hiding my ignorance in neurolinguistic-cum-philosophical psychobabble. My eyes stare reflectively into some distant space. And, after a few thoughtful moments of reflection, I say something to the effect of: "My experience with English, as your experience with your language, is so ingrained in my mind that it has become automatic. I never have to think about using a passive versus an active or the past perfect versus a simple past. I never have to think about which article to use. I 'just do it!'" That satisfies them for the few seconds it takes to furrow their brows, cock their heads to one side, and scrunch their lips as if to say, "What kind of linguistic-cum-philosophical psychobabble is that, anyway? It would have been better if you had said, 'It's because the sky is a nice shade of Carolina blue, and the grass is greener on the other side.'"

And so, after many years of perfecting the art of the reflective far-off stare and the deep linguistic responses that spring from it, my old age and deepened maturity have taught me to refrain from such answers because they do sound like empty-headed psycho-goop. Aside from that, they are rather patronizing. But most important, those who have thought about the confounded nature of English grammar, and have taken the time to formulate a thoughtful question, are actually interested in knowing the answer, even if my response is about as precise as a mountain landscape in an early-morning fog. But I have grown quite fond of the questions, not because it provides me with the opportunity to say something profound, but because the questions are, more times than not, insightful, and because, again more times than not, they strike at the heart of how our language and our culture interact. And given an appropriate and thoughtful answer that is not too laden with gobbledygook, I just might be able to help them (and me) understand how difficult English is sometimes, especially given the variety of contexts in which they find themselves on a regular basis, especially the ones firmly ensconced in and around my home university in the southern Appalachian Mountains. I have a great appreciation for these questions, and those who ask them, because they seem to lie at the heart of how people acquire language, or at least I think so.

Students ask run-of-the-mill questions like, "What is the difference between can and may?" Sometimes they ask mindbenders like, "What does the perfect tense mean and when do you use it?" "Do you have a subjunctive in English like we do in Spanish?" "What does it look like and when do you use it?" On the surface, such questions seem to have strict formulaic answers. However, for many speakers of American English, it is not so cut and dried at all. The beauty of reflecting on questions like these is that they unlock some of the secrets of who we are as a speech community, and wider, as a culture. They reflect a bit about our history as an immigrant people from many lands far and wide. More importantly, they permit me as a teacher to gain a bit of insight into how my students are undertaking the complex task of learning English, what hypotheses they are making about the language, and how they are resolving their hypotheses with real-life contextualized English. Besides that, these questions are fun to ponder.

My research for this book would not have been possible without the inquisitive students in my English for internationals classes. For two decades now, they have provided me with why-questions in the contexts of numerous real-world conversations with native speakers from a variety of dialects. They have sent me searching for answers which, in some cases, still evade me. But, in turn, they have provided me with many a eureka moment, in which case I have gained a better understanding of how my native language interacts in my native culture. This serves as the rationale for this handbook. Within the text, I offer numerous salient examples from my years in teaching that class. These examples will usually be expressed in the first person.

This book attempts to tackle these notoriously difficult "why" questions. Rather than focus on the grammar of literacy, it focuses on common-usage speech, and seeks to explain why English speakers articulate the way they do. This book also helps the reader understand the cultural dimensions involved in the grammatical choices speakers make. It makes use of the latest insights from neuroscience, an area that longstanding ESL grammar textbooks have yet to tap. While striving to be detailed, it avoids the highly technical jargon of many other works about grammar. What is more, this text is, by extension, about how we teach language; how we enable students to make effective snap judgments about the context in which they often find themselves, snap judgments about cultures with which they might not be familiar, and snap judgments about language. I ask the reader to keep in mind, of course, that first, American English is a vast hodgepodge of almost ungeneralizable dialects and registers, and second, American English is continually changing and adapting to cultural changes.

This book is primarily intended as a handbook for ESL teachers. It is also a supplemental text for students enrolled in Teaching English as a Second Language. It is not intended to replace such seminal textbooks as Pat Byrd and Beverly Benson's *Applied English Grammar* (especially useful for international students of English who need additional work in writing academic-style English), nor Marianne Celce-Murcia and Diane Larsen-Freeman's *The Grammar Book* (which, while being the gold standard in the field, can sometimes be overwhelming in its scope, and appears outdated in its theoretical approach).

The text is organized into four parts. First comes a general introduction, followed by a chapter about neuroscience concepts important to the later chapters. Chapters 2 through 5 cover articles, prepositions, the subjunctive, gerunds and infinitives. Chapters 6 through 11 deal with negatives, interrogatives, imperatives, passives, modals, and temporal expressions. Following all is a conclusion.

Introduction

GRAMMAR

What is meant by grammar in this guide may not be what is conventionally meant by grammar. First of all, there is a marked distinction between the **grammar of literacy**, namely the art of using language to construct coherent and sometimes even inspired writing, and the **grammar of common usage**, how speakers actually use the language in everyday speech. Grammarians like James Kilpatrick and William Safire have made distinguished careers out of commenting on the subject of the how to write coherently and cogently, i.e., the grammar of literacy. There is no reason to even pretend to provide the reader with as informed a discourse as Mr. Kilpatrick regularly supplied in his column. So this book will leave you to consult his writings and the many tomes of learned others about the subject of the grammar of literacy, except for one broad stroke which is pertinent to the discussion now and will be pertinent later. And that is, those who are in the English teaching business often confuse the two conventions of grammar, insisting that the principles that are common in literacy are completely appropriate to those of common usage. While having the skills to write and speak in what the wider culture believes is an "educated" manner, and while the insistence on learning a more standardized variety of English, if there truly is such a thing, is beneficial to circumvent the prejudices against certain dialects, the fact remains that, despite our tireless efforts and increasingly higher levels of education, many people continually, and quite automatically, say things like, "There are less people doing that now," or "Me and Wanda went to that party last night," and "Where are you at?" and "As for my family and myself, I don't think I'll go to that restaurant again."

This conflict between the grammar of literacy and the grammar of common usage gives rise to a great amount of confusion about notions of correctness, what rules speakers should follow, and so forth. Teacher-trainees sometimes ask why so many speakers of English speak English incorrectly, and in my own classroom I consistently have to remind them that speakers of English do speak English correctly in everyday conversation. While there is a general set of conventions about what is appropriate grammatical speech and what is not, decisions about what is correct and what is incorrect are often made on the basis of factors other than grammatical conventions. Native speakers may begin a sentence by talking about something, and then immediately change topics without noting where they want the conversation to go. They may stutter, not in the sense of the medical condition, but in the sense that the word they want to use is right on the tips of their tongues and not coming out of their mouths. They sometimes stumble over subject-verb agreement or dangle a preposition or even split an infinitive. But all-in-all, native-speaker speech is pretty nigh perfect. What is more, the way native speakers say things or do not say things has very little to do with the seemingly countless hours of boring repetitive drills or the sentence diagramming all of them had to endure in their middle and high school classes. Rather, the sentences native speakers utter seem as natural to them and, at least most of the time, to the listeners as walking or riding a bicycle. To qualify that a bit, native speech may sound like music to the ears of a listener who speaks the same dialect, and rather much like fingernails screeching over a blackboard to those who do not speak the same dialect. Therefore, this discussion will be limited to the grammar of common usage.

Grammar of Common Usage

What exactly is the grammar of common usage? **Grammar can be defined as the scaffold (the superstructure) by which a person is able to express perspectives and co-create meaning with another person within a particular speech community.** When speakers express themselves to one another, it is commonly their intent to convey meaning to the person with whom they are conversing, unless they want to be intentionally obscure or unless they want to outright lie. In other words, they want the other person to see, albeit metaphorically, the images they have in their heads, the perspectives that have been constantly shaped and reshaped by experience. And they want the other person to understand their perspectives as they understand them, or close enough at least so that the listener can get the idea. Grammar, as well as other verbal and non-verbal cues such as context and gestures, among others, allow people to be transparent enough for others to understand, at least most of the time, and allow the circles of individual perspectives to intersect.

So the theme of this book is, how does grammar operate in everyday life, in everyday speech, among everyday people? How are speakers of language, in the blink of an eye, capable of processing events, and then constructing appropriate language as a response? At its heart, this book is about that blink of an eye, that process so well described by Malcolm Gladwell in his book, *Blink*. What is the process of linguistic "thin slicing," that selective nuanced attention that is essential for understanding and communication?

TEACHING GRAMMAR

In the past two or three decades, with the advent of new approaches to language teaching, especially those that heavily emphasize communicative proficiency, explicit and comprehensive grammar instruction, methodologies *en vogue* in the 1950s and 1960s have largely gone the way of the eight-track tape or the Sony Walkman (although, as a 2006 study by Connie Zucker pointed out, there is still a tendency among many teachers to "treat grammar as a course content rather than as a means to an end").[1] Modern functional approaches in linguistics, and the pedagogies that follow from them, stress the importance of exposing learners to naturally-occurring speech in various contexts, the goal of which is to enable learners to gain communicative competence. Rote grammatical drills which ask students to inflect verb forms or fill in the correct preposition have been replaced by collaborative classroom activities where learners engage each other and the instructor in conversations about everyday topics in the target language. While the correction of performance errors is still considered an important function of pedagogy, corrections are made by modeling the proper form/discourse in order for the student to form the correct hypothesis about the form in the appropriate context. ESL researchers Simon Borg and Anna Burns have confirmed this trend in a 2008 study. Their study showed that ESL teachers tend to avoid direct instruction of grammar, preferring to integrate grammatical instruction within the functional context of the topic at hand. Other studies, such as by Davis (2009), Antonio (2005), Kettle (2000) and Lukin (1994), reinforce the notion that the most effective learning occurs when grammatical structures are grounded within readily understood contexts, for language learners seem not to, as more generative approaches insist, acquire language piecemeal. Rather, language is acquired in chunks, grammar melded with context.

Two of the more interesting recent contributions to the field, and which deserve a special mention here as supports to this text, are one by Richard Cullen in 2008, and an article by Margaret Kettle in 2000. Professor Cullen, influenced by Henry Widdowson's notion of "grammar as a liberating force," argues for an approach to grammatical instruction in which learners are increasingly aware of the choices of grammatical forms they have within any given linguistic discourse. Kettle stresses the importance of acquiring whole discourses in which lexical items and grammar have particular meaning, rather than disparate individual lexical items and grammatical rules devoid of context. These two studies, as well as those cited earlier, lend credence to the approach of this text, and confirm the need for pedagogical resources that attempt to explain how grammar functions in common usage; thus, the rationale for this handbook.

1
The Mascagni Effect[1]

A short scenario, captured on video, illustrates the importance of the interface between discourse and the construction of grammar in conversational situations. The scenario begins with a young man and woman, both college-age, sitting at a table in a coffee shop somewhere engaged in a lively conversation. At first, they appear mismatched. He is dressed in all black, sports lip and nose rings, and has what appears to be an ankh tattooed on his neck. She is pretty, dressed conservatively, and has no visible piercings save the small gold balls in her earlobes. They are both drinking coffee, and because there is no sound, they could be discussing practically anything from school to music to who they think is the odds-on favorite to win the World Cup.

    The fifteen native speakers of English, all studying to become teachers of this perplexing language, are watching this short video in a modern English grammar class. The sound has been turned off, so the only identifiable cues the students have to rely upon are the context and the conversants' non-verbal language, including facial, hand and body gestures, the proximal distance between them as the conversation waxes and wanes, and the maintenance of eye contact. Periodically, the professor stops the film and asks what is happening, all in an attempt to explain prepositions, in this case *on* and *above*, more specifically, where the interlocutors' coffee cups are with respect to the table. At various points in the video, the interlocutors are holding their coffee cups *above* the table. At other times, the coffee cups are resting *on* the table. When asked, the students respond appropriately vis-à-vis the position of the coffee cups and the table; that is, they respond from their understanding of what *above* and *on* mean in the given context of the spatial relationship between two objects. The understanding of this spatial relationship has been acquired and honed over time, and is deeply seated in one's cultural understanding of *above* vs. *on*.

The same video was shown to a group of fifteen students from Japan in an English for internationals class. As was the case with the group of native–English speakers, the goal was to assess the students' understanding of the spatial relationship of the coffee cups and the table, and how to mark that relationship in language. Pausing the video at the point where the coffee cups are resting on the table, the professor asks the class where the coffee cups are. The class unanimously agrees that the cups are on the table. Then, the professor pauses the video of the same two people enjoying their coffee, engaged in the same conversation, but this time each holding their cups off the surface of the table while leaning over the table. But this time, when the professor asks, "Where is the cup?", the Japanese students unanimously agree that the cup is still on the table.

"How could this be?" the professor asks. "I can see that a space exists between the cup and the table. And in my perspective, the cup is above the table."

But while the students agree that there is a distance between the cups and the table, and despite the professor's urging to the contrary, the Japanese students still insists that the cup is *on* the table. In Japanese, one would say *Copu ga taberu no ue ni arimasu* ("The cup is on the table"), whether or not the cup is physically touching the table. As long as the cup has not broken the vertical plane of the table, it is still *on* the table.

So what is the answer? How is a cup both on and above the table at the same time? The answer is a complicated one, integrating language, culture and being, and one's sense of oneself in one's surroundings. There is even some evidence, albeit anecdotal, that while many speakers of Japanese and speakers of languages in the Sino-Tibetan family physically "see" the space between the cup and table, they do not "visualize" it, because, in their perspectives, the plane of the table extends beyond its horizontal surface. That is to say, they likely possess a different notion of how parts of something interact with the whole picture, and thus visualize their relationship differently. The same process is evident when a professor asks Japanese students if a picture is on the wall. "Yes," they respond, "and the wall is on the picture" (each participating in the other's being). Speakers of English would probably find this idea totally baffling.

For all who saw the young man and woman holding their cups above the table, there is no doubt that the space between the table and cup actually exists. But, for those whose native language is English, they actually both "see" it and "visualize" the space as important. That visualization comes from having seen cups above tables in multiple contexts. And whenever they have seen cups above tables, etc., the concept of *above*, one that is learned very early, is reinforced. Further, because the relationship between cup and table has been established in this context, and they are able to describe that relationship, the description further influences their perspectives, and so on recursively. This process is called Hybridized Perspective. What this book means by that is that perspectives are continually shaped by experiences in particular contexts. So when people see something, they not only perceive it with their eyes as an object in space, they also interpret it through the lenses of culture and experience. Perspectives are constantly changing, hybridizing.

Language

The extraordinary responses of groups of Asian students over the years helped prompt an essential question: What is language and what role does it play in the interaction between people? Is it, as some have argued, a unique and particular neuro-biological system? If so, what kind of system is it? Is it a knowledge-based system, a rule-based grammar? Or is it a performance-based system, a complex set of motor skills responding to the input of a complex set of stimuli? Or is it both kinds of systems? Moreover, is it even possible to separate language components from non-language elements since advances in neuroscience have demonstrated the close connection between neural networks, the boundaries of which are often more fuzzy-edged than hard and fast?

Historically reductionist definitions of language, such as one suggested by Chomsky, that "language is a set of sentences each finite in length and constructed out of a finite set of elements," can be unsatisfying. Wider definitions such as the one proposed by Raymond Williams, who pointed out that language is a "definition of human beings in the world," inspire more comfort. This book favors the wider approach and defines language as the communicative/interactive expression of hybridized perspective.

Language involves a complex system of highly specialized networks in both hemispheres of the human brain, with two areas in the left hemisphere (for a majority of people), Broca's area (located mid-temple) and Wernicke's area (just above the ear) serving as primary integrative relay centers. Language is a distributive, overlapping set of neural structures, receiving input from other neural systems such as vision, audition, primary and secondary motor systems, and systems devoted to higher-order functions like interpretation and emotion. Language can be envisioned much like a spider web, sending fibers in many directions, tying into existing systems with the centers of the web being Broca's and Wernicke's areas. In this system, there is constant feedback, adapting to the changing goals and intentions of an event, and the ever-changing flow of linguistic discourse.

LIVING LARGE

So where does grammar fit in to all this? In the introduction of this text, grammar was described as the scaffold (the superstructure) by which a person is able to express perspectives and co-create meaning with another person within a particular speech community. This definition of grammar is a bit different from the usual traditional rule-based ones most have been exposed to in languages classes. For many years now, some professors have chafed at the more traditional approaches of grammatical analysis/instruction which view grammar long on form and weak on function, a set of discrete rules with obvious exceptions. Even some contemporary linguistic approaches, which appropriately consider the interconnection between real-world information and language structure, still fall short of analytical "elegance" due in large part to the widespread insistence that language is reducible to narrowly-defined component systems of phonemes, morphemes, syntax, and semantics (add now pragmatics to the list of minimal components). While these new approaches fare somewhat better than more traditional ones, the rub is that language is significantly more complex, as are the speakers who use it, than most linguistic theories allow, and will assuredly defy the most determined efforts to pigeonhole it.

This is not to say that language cannot undergo some level of analysis, nor is this to suggest that no linguistic generalizations are possible. This is to simply point out that the definitions that have served linguistics sufficiently in the past are no longer adequate, especially in light of recent discoveries in neuroscience. Thus, apart from illustrating how output components of language are sequenced, sentence diagramming won't get one very far in understanding the meaning of the Appalachian expression, "Let's go to the house." Neither will the seemingly rote learning of grammar rules and the overuse of dialogues in a "let's go to the bank, post office, you-name-the-place" curriculum. Neither will simply speaking German, Spanish, or French in an American classroom without somehow transforming that classroom into Germany/Austria, or one of the many Spanish-speaking or French-speaking cultures wherein the many nuances of language are contextualized. Perhaps the rub is generated by the lack of adequate new methodologies to get at what language is and how it interacts with experiential and cultural knowledge in the human brain. It is a rub that will sadly continue until new technologies enable people to "see" more clearly what is going on inside our heads when we communicate with each other.

Here is an example which serves to illustrate this inadequacy. In a linguistics classes a long time ago, when a more strict version of generative grammar was very much in vogue, a student was given a sentence that was not supposed to be possible in English. The sentence was, "Mary solved the building." The sentence was not possible because it defied what at that time were called "semantic co-occurrence restrictions." That is, somewhere in the semantic component of the class's linguistic knowledge module, "solve" and "building" cannot go together. While it is true that this utterance in and of itself makes little sense, the reason it makes little sense is not because of a semantic co-occurrence failure, but that the sentence would probably never be uttered by speakers without at least some kind of clearly defined context. While "Mary solved the building" is not supposed to be a possible English sentence, if the truth be known, a world in which this sentence makes some sense can be conceived.

Here's how. Suppose one of the new buildings on the (fictional) Pembrotanck University campus has just been completed. It opens to great fanfare. There are new spacious faculty offices with the latest equipment and supplies and at least 10 "smart" classrooms on every floor. It's quiet and even plush. Unfortunately, six months after opening, a sizable crack appears in one of the outside walls. The original architect is called in, the contractor is called in, and both are baffled by this crack in the wall that is not supposed to be there. And so the design team works on the problem for a month without success. They simply cannot solve the building! So the architect calls one of her colleagues, a crackerjack engineer named Mary Smalling from Georgia Tech. She agrees to have a look at it, comes to Pembrotanck, runs a series of tests, and discovers that one of the load-bearing walls is .002 millimeters off where it is supposed to be. Moreover, she determines that the crack will not get any worse, that all that is needed is to patch the crack, and, for extra safety, put a series of decorative, load-bearing columns next to the wall. Everyone is delighted, the design team, Pembrotanck officials, students and faculty, everyone. As the design team is departing, the architect who had originally suggested that Dr. Smalling consult, is overheard to say, "Good day's work. Mary solved the building, and we can all get on with our other projects!"

First, apologies to civil engineers, architects and contractors for such a simplistic and purely amateurish example. But the point is, what makes the utterance "Mary solved the building" possible is the necessary and, save neurological injury or illness, ingrained link between contextual and cultural information, experience, memory, emotion and language.

Now, one might say, "Well, when we say 'Mary solved the building,' we assume that Mary solved a particular problem the building posed." True enough. But the possibility remains that, given the right context, one can say "Mary solved the building" and be understood by others. Moreover, what makes the utterance understandable is not because of some hidden linguistic trace, a concealed word under the surface somewhere. What makes "Mary solved the building" understandable is that the people involved share enough knowledge, have similar enough experiences, to know what it means.

A second and very much related rub is the idea that the linguistics world has conceived of language as this almost mysterious distinct entity, a self-contained component located somewhere in the midst of Broca's and Wernicke's areas of the left hemisphere of the brain, modular in nature and analyzable as a particular neurocognitive phenomenon quite apart from other neurocognitive phenomena. While there is overwhelming evidence that Broca's and Wernicke's areas have important language functions, forming a centralized relay system, as it were, responsible for linguistic processing and production, there is some evidence to suggest that language as a holistic process traverses into neural territories not commonly associated with language knowledge. These neural territories, called the association cortices, are not widely researched for their role in linguistic processing and production. Yet, it is these neural networks that play a vital role in language, a role which is connectional in nature.

Some traditional definitions of language delineate various levels of linguistic phenomena, one of which is morphology, which is often defined as the study of morphemes, which are the minimal units of grammatical meaning in a language. And while there is little difficulty with the existence of morphemes in general nor with this definition, language should be analyzed in a broader scope; that is, while the morpheme can be spoken of as defining the minimal unit of grammatical meaning in language, the minimal unit of meaning in language is not in fact a small structure like a morpheme or a sentence, for that matter, but rather a larger unit, Discourse.

There are several factors supporting this. First, although linguists have customarily approached language research from the level of the morpheme as the building block of the sentence as primary unit for analysis (at least they have since Chomsky), analyzing single words or sentences without a broader context is akin to being plopped down in the middle of New York City and trying to find Guido's place without an address. The second factor is that if language can be reduced down to its minimal component unit, the morpheme, why not continue the reduction, down to phonemes, down to individual action potentials in the primary motor cortex? How minimal is minimal?

Discourse

So if it is difficult to analyze language in minimal units smaller than discourse, how is discourse defined? For this discussion, this book distinguishes two levels of discourse: Macro-Level Discourse and Linguistic Discourse.

The French philosopher Michel Foucault classifies the term "discourse" as "bodies of knowledge." He further defines "bodies of knowledge" as "a set of conditions which enable and constrain imagination."[2] For Foucault, the question of whether or not something is real is not the issue. What is at issue is that the real world, or better, consciousness of it, effects how people represent it. If something is conceivable in the real world, then it is possible to be discoursed. Naturally, not everything can be discoursed. It depends on the extent of both historical and social knowledge. He further goes on to say that discourse is comprised of enunciations and statements, although enunciations and statements are not technically units of discourse as morphemes and sentences are said to be units of language. Enunciations are those things which can be said and thought. There are only a limited number of linguistic structures that can be put together in particular ways. So language is limited. Statements include both linguistic elements and non-verbal expression. Both reflect components of our knowledge system.

Following from Foucault's definition of discourse, Macro-Level Discourse can be likened to context, the various socio-historical, political, and cultural conditions that make up our daily lives. Linguistic Discourse is what actually happens when people use spoken, written or signed language, and combine it with non-verbal elements to facilitate communication.

Discourse has many properties. Discourse is self-repeating, ever-changing, reflective of variations in psychological and physical contexts. Discourse involves seeing, hearing, word-recognition/meaning, abstract conceptualization, memory, emotion. Discourse involves the continual processing of cultural memory and ongoing events. In other words, discourse is, to use a word borrowed from neuroscience, pluripotential, that is, capable of multiple interpretations.

To illustrate, here is an example from own of my own classes. Although some of my in-class comments, both wise and inane, have been met with a sentence or a grunt or worse, I am quite certain there is something bigger behind that sentence or grunt, a whole meaningful discourse. For example, one day, while teaching my graduate linguistics class, I made the assertion, "Discourse is the minimal unit of meaning in language." Besides the puzzled looks garnered by such an assertion, one young man sitting at the edge of the semicircle issued what sounded like a rather disdainful grunt that resembled the "humph" that you might get when you say something totally off the wall. Amused by this, and fully expecting at least one "humph," I later asked the young man what he was thinking when he "humphed." He told me in great detail that my assertion held a great deal of interest to him, especially since it was totally contrary to everything he had learned in linguistics. He indicated that discourse was a performance phenomenon and that we do not "know" discourse. He had heard that we do know the meaning of morphemes as part of "knowledge" of words. But as he got to thinking about it, he realized that it is very difficult to know exactly what a morpheme means outside of the discourse in which it is used. I was astounded by the extent and detail of his explanation. In fact, I was astounded on three accounts. First, I was impressed by the thoroughness with which this student came to the conclusion about my definition. Second, although his response to me was a self-contained utterance, a sentence as it were, "humph," there was obviously a complex discourse behind it, which indicates that he was not "humphing" on a simple sentential level. And third, I just plain misinterpreted the "humph." It took his extended explanation for me to understand that the "humph" was not a disdainful or even skeptical "humph," but that it was a genuine investigatory "humph." The point was made. The student's "humph" needed sufficient discourse to give it meaning, a point illustrated earlier with the strange case of "Mary solved the building."

One of the principle reasons for the claim that discourse is the minimal unit of meaning in language has to do with the latest research into the nature of language and the brain. Recent findings in the areas of neurocognition and neurolinguistics seem to point toward a more holistic view of the role language plays in thought and emotion. Neurobiology is teaching marvelous new things about the way the brain works, confirming a few notions and tossing out many preconceived ideas. For instance, neuroscientists have discovered that language and learning are far more complicated processes than previously believed. In fact, a person has billions of neurons that carry multiple functions from enabling one to have a steady heart rate and to breathe regularly to remembering the face of one's spouse.

These billions of neurons cannot work alone. The information in human brains is organized as highly complex and interrelated networks by which one learns. These networks are comprised of Declarative Memory (explicit facts such as a telephone number, definition of words like "go," memories of events, and so on) and Procedural Memory (implicit memories of things one knows how to do, knowledge of how to apply one thing to another, and general problem-solving strategies). The process of language learning is about getting information that is explored in class into these complex networks of long-term memory, and making that information permanent and automatic. What a task!

University of Southern California neurologist Antonio Damasio has demonstrated that far from being a completely localized-modular phenomenon, language is activated in many areas of the left hemisphere of the brain depending upon the function of the language, and that "literacy," i.e., reading and writing, is processed differently and in different although somewhat overlapping locales than spoken language.[3] Moreover, there is mounting evidence that every brain operates a little differently.

According to Damasio, our knowledge and understanding of new information occur when this new material engages with our emotional memories. Learning occurs most efficiently when learners become emotionally engaged with the material being taught. New information has to connect with old information, something already familiar, a process termed "scaffolding." Learning can be delayed or stopped if there is little connection between what has already been established in long-term memory, familiar to our personal experiences and memories, and information presented anew.

Damasio's theory has significant applications to second-language teaching and learning; that is, the importance of linking new information to contexts that are immediately recognizable.[4]

Language acquisition has to do with patterned relationships, experience within a defined cultural context. The brain is an efficient categorizer and connector, linking new information with information already learned and accessible with a person's sense of self.

Harvard psychiatrist John Ratey suggests that, for most people, language is a function of the left hemisphere.[5] But for some, the right hemisphere is predominant, while still others are ambihemispheric, a bit like being ambidextrous. He also shows that while Broca's area and Wernicke's area are intimately involved in language, language functions are widely spread throughout the left hemisphere (for most people) involving: the limbic system, especially the anterior cingulate gyrus, that part of the brain responsible for memory, learning, and emotion; and the prefrontal cortex, the area of the brain associated with complex cognition, critical thinking and decision-making, and personality. Professor Ratey's suggestion that neuro-grammar (meaning the development of grammatical form and function in the brain) is located in several sites gives rise to a novel theory that high-order neural networks which contain pieces of one's vast experience may also have the grammar necessary to represent them in language.

Another likely possibility, one that has great potential and merits closer investigation, is that these grammatical networks are in close proximity to what Antonio Damasio calls convergence zones. In Damasio's words, "Convergence zones located in the prefrontal cortices are thus the repository of dispositional representations for the appropriately categorized and unique contingencies of our life experiences."[6] Bits of information converge at lightning speed. Near these convergence zones are networks devoted to grammatical form and function which enable the convergence of information and emotion to be expressed linguistically.

Professor George Ojemann of the University of Washington in Seattle has demonstrated that there is no one language center in the brain.[7] Rather, speech sites vary from person to person. Professor Ojemann's conclusion is that language is not a single function within the human brain, but that many regions of the brain are working in parallel. Findings by neurologist James Austin support this viewpoint. Austin views the brain as a "unified system of attention" where there is interaction between the left and right hemispheres. The right hemisphere "knows objects, discerns emotions and links non-verbal cues with verbal ones."[8] Likewise, the left hemisphere is "adept at the story line, picks out salient details." The production and processing of language occur with a "meeting of the minds," as it were: a connection between hemispheres.

Why is it that some students shine and some barely glimmer? Why is it that it takes some students countless hours to get the difference between the prepositions "on" and "in," as in Mary rides "in a boat" and "on the cruise ship," while some get it in no time?

Neuroscientists are beginning to understand a relatively newly-recognized phenomenon called Long-Term Potentiation, or LTP. Important to the discussion of grammar is that LTP is the process by which one learns new things and is able to retrieve them with lightning speed. (A thorough discussion of LTP would delve into the nature of the synaptic transfer of glutamate and the intricate workings of the hippocampus.)

Here's how it happens. A neuron is stimulated over and over and over, and that overstimulation causes an electrical response, making the neuron "stronger," that is, more likely to receive information, hold that information, and retrieve it later. That explains why, for example, when a professor has been trying to get students from France to say "this" rather than "zees," it is practiced over and over until the students are blue in the face, and suddenly one day, Jean Yves starts making the "th" sound as if he had been making it all his life. That explains why two students from Hong Kong, after countless hours of demonstration and practice, can now write beautiful, coherent English discourse.

Much of this process is quite non-linear. It works faster for some than for others. But that's the way it works. And what is more, and this is equally exciting, it seems to work better in moderately stressful situations — not a lot of stress, mind you, but just enough to release certain hormones, called — for those who are interested in the science — glucocorticoids. One would not want too much of the stuff. Too much blocks the LTP process as, arguably, does too much alcohol, MSG, or, controversially, aspartame. So much for the argument that it is good to get a bit drunk before speaking another language, following the old language-learning adage that a few beers will bring out the best in your language abilities. It's just not so, although one may be less inhibited, which is a good thing in terms of language learning. Ideally, one would want just enough healthy stimulation and moderate amounts of stress to accentuate LTP. How is that pulled off? That seems to be the million-dollar question because it's a matter of the individual. Somehow there needs to be the right amount of stress, repeated stimulation, and the right associations to tap into the appropriate neural networks for it to happen most effectively.

But even with all the tools available, and with all the exciting knowledge recently gained, currently, there is no available neurolinguistic methodology which exists to test this interface between what are commonly considered language areas and the association cortices of the brain. The technology may arguably be a decade or two away. However, slowly and surely, experts are getting there. There are new neuro-imagers, the functional magnetic resonance imaging (fMRI) being one, which have real-time stereoscopic capabilities. These new machines are not only more efficient, but are getting smaller as well. Whereas with the older imagers, a patient had to be force-fed into a claustrophobia-inducing tube, new technology is allowing patients to be seated in relative comfort while relatively portable imagers capture synaptic processes in real time. Unfortunately, the technology is still in its infancy and is unbelievably expensive. And so researchers are left with only a partial explanation of how language is constructed and processed synaptically. Neurolinguists can both explore neurological deficiencies in human brains with increasing accuracy and report, again with increasing accuracy, the linguistic consequences of such neural defects. At best, however, neurolinguists must still project, backward or forward, how "normal" brains would function given no neural defects. In the race for answers, the technology still lags behind the questions. It will catch up, but sadly, while one can speculate on the synaptic nature of contextualized conversation, theories such as the one presented here continue to remain untested, and will remain so for many years to come.

Perhaps what is needed most is a new methodology for getting at this important question. Even then, one major hurdle remains. Even if researchers are able to capture the various synaptic processes of human conversation in videoscopic images, even if they are able to snap an image to represent human communication, those contextual, notably human components of interaction which influence grammatical choice will still require analysis, an analysis which is qualitative and sometimes imprecise. One would still have to consider the complexities of culture, of competing and often conflicting values and modes of behavior. The value of group memberships, the consistency of in- and out-groups as well as societal roles, will have to be compared and analyzed. One would still have to account for factors of personality and environment which are not so neatly nor easily measured. A holistic view of grammar must take all of these factors into consideration, not just ones we for which can derive easily calculable data. This dilemma has consistently been one of the essential problems with linguistic analysis. Linguistics at best is a quasi-science, and its methodologies are "messy" when held up to the rigor of traditional scientific methodologies. So, for at least the foreseeable future, the task of accurately answering the "whys" of grammatical form and function remains difficult.

One might ask at this point, if scientists are still far from answering how this process works, how can professors and teachers possibly know what they are doing in the language classroom? What does this have to do with the students, young and old, who sit wide-eyed and enthusiastic in language classrooms? Everything! If the neurobiologists are correct, and there is ample evidence to suggest that they are, language students, no matter what their level of proficiency, would need a learning environment which would produce the right amounts of stimulation, stress and associations to learn the target language, however defined, most effectively. This happens most elegantly in the context of life, and additionally, in those contexts in classrooms where real-life contextualized communication is happening, where person contacts person.

Here is a real-life example of where learning may fail and where it may succeed. The first scenario is the recipe for disaster.

When a Spanish-speaking worker named Pedro (not his real name) arrived in Boone, North Carolina, he was met by a cacophony of noise which seemed to be gibberish, when in fact it was English. Questions were asked of him. In the grocery store, checking out: "Paper or plastic?" At the Hardee's: "Would you like to try one of our combo specials today? It comes with biggie fries."

On the job, when working at a local resort, he had to perform a complicated landscaping task that involved trimming trees around a set of power lines. The job foreman called the landscapers in for training on this particular job. The foreman, an English speaker, explained the task in English, and — not trained in the particular needs of non-native speakers — explained the task using technical language, and he spoke quickly. Then he asked if Pedro had any questions. Pedro shook his head "no" even though he had not understood. He did not want to put his job in jeopardy by seeming not to know what was going on. In this case, there was much too much stimulation for someone who was a novice in English. There was much too much stress. Pedro found himself in situations where he had to respond to particular questions aimed directly at him without the equipment to handle the questions. And there were few associations made. The person at the checkout usually does not point to paper bags nor plastic bags. Neither does the Hardees employee make visual reference to the particular combo in question, and I'm sure Pedro had never before been asked if he wanted to "biggie" anything. The job scenario became more dangerous because Pedro did not understand the task. So Pedro was forced to make an association from vocabulary he had never heard, and with grammar with which he was not familiar. It was one big cacophony! Pedro does not learn in that situation. LTP does not happen, even if Pedro happens to figure some of it out, learns how to do the job like the boss wants, and gets the biggie fries.

Now, for the recipe for success, here is another job scenario. The landscaping crew on which Pedro worked was out mowing and weed-eating a road right-of-way. Their tractor broke down and the other crew members could not fix the tractor. Pedro, being an auto mechanic, volunteered to take a look at the problem. Seeing the problem was bigger than one person could handle, he elicited his coworkers to help him out. Now, the situation was such that Pedro was in charge, and despite having language difficulties, he knew what the problem was and how to fix it. The stress level was appropriate; there was just enough to raise the levels of glucocorticoids in the brain, but not so much that LTP was blocked.

What is more, Pedro could make the appropriate associations as needed. He could ask a coworker to hand him a particular tool, even if he did not know the word, by miming the word or pointing and asking, "How do you say?" Do this enough because of faulty equipment as a result of budget cuts, or use that particular tool enough or do that process enough, and Pedro will likely learn how to negotiate the process in English. Those neurons become "supercharged," and he does not lose it! So now the boss promoted him to maintain the equipment. He now keeps the trucks, tractors, weed-eaters, log splitters, etc., in working order, and when he needs help, he shows others how to do the task needed. Pedro has learned! The "whys" have become "because."

ON D.I.P.P.S. AND D.O.M.P.S.

If language is a linked system, interacting with other major neural systems, what then are its components? While linguistic initial input and final output consists of patterned sounds, words, structure and meaning, this book proposes that language as a neural system has only two components which continuously interact and feed back to each other. This book refers to these two components as D.I.P.P.S. (Discoursal Input Perceptual Processing System) and D.O.M.P.S. (Discoursal Output Motor Production System).

D.I.P.P.S. is integrated into neural systems responsible for vision, audition, and somato-sensation, as well as higher-order cognitive systems responsible for meaning, event processing, memory and the theory of self. D.O.M.P.S. is integrated into cortical systems responsible for motor production and control, memory, and learning, and both Broca's and Wernicke's areas. And D.I.P.P.S. is integrated into D.O.M.P.S. and vice versa.

It works like this. Suppose, for example, a friend of yours has just asked you to go camping in one of the parks along the Blue Ridge Parkway. You are delighted by the invitation because you have had the experience of camping along the Parkway, and that experience was completely pleasurable. So you accept the invitation and add, "I just love camping on the Parkway!" Notice here you have a choice of saying, "I just love camping on the Parkway," or "I just love to camp on the Parkway," a choice between using two different grammatical forms, a gerund or an infinitive. You choose the gerund. Now this choice is instantaneous. But if Damasio is right, and language is a part of our extended consciousness, then the choice between using a gerund or an infinitive is a "conscious" decision (maybe intentional is better), albeit one of which you are not overtly aware. That "decision" occurs far too quickly to register in your awareness. Further, it is a decision modeled, learned and used in varying contexts recursively (perhaps another term is needed for this neurological function — one which encompasses intention and assessment in nanoseconds). But "decide" you do, and the choice matters, that is, your intention — or Motivational Valence — matters. The contention is that the two grammatical forms, one using the gerund and the other using the infinitive, do not mean the same thing in the context of the discourse about camping on the Blue Ridge.

When your friend asked you to go camping, you immediately remembered the experience of camping on the Parkway. In fact for a moment, the neural activation of experiential networks allowed you to "remember" the experience as if you were living it at that very moment. You were "on" the Parkway, watching the morning mist of summer rise above Price Lake, the air crisp, the sun beginning to rise over the rounded peaks. You "remembered" the feelings connected with the experience. You remembered feeling relaxed and content, grateful for being away from the office for awhile. These memories with their associated emotions flooded your consciousness. And you wanted to express this experience in language to your friend. Bits and pieces of the experience come together in one or more convergence zones, which link to proximate grammatical networks, which correspond with both the content and emotional value of the experience. Given that the emotional content of your collected memory is strong and positive, and given that gerunds are used in emotive expressions like this, you say, "I just love camping in the mountains."

The Importance of Culture

Perhaps the most important and compelling reason to argue that discourse is the minimal unit of meaning in language has to do with the importance of culture in grammatical decisions. Decisions do not mean time-consuming, overtly conscious decisions, as in, "I would rather buy the Porsche than the Subaru." Rather, decisions of this nature occur on the neural level. As indicated earlier, "decision" may be too strong a term. It is more a contextual evaluation performed in a matter of milliseconds. What is more, culture intimately matters in these neural evaluations. One's understanding and, especially, one's experience of culture in both its broadest and narrowest terms enables one to negotiate the world, and utilize the grammar necessary to effectively communicate.

Human language does not happen in the vacuum of a context-free environment. In fact, human language as it is used for communication is filtered through a number of intricate networks of contextually-based experiences. Intercultural communication specialists William Gudykunst and

Young Yun Kim distinguish four such filters, which they term cultural, sociocultural, psychocultural and environmental.

Cultural Variables

Although culture can be defined broadly, Gudykunst and Kim view this cultural filter narrowly to include such matters as worldview, values, choices (which they call pattern variables), ends and means.[9] They contend that when two or more people communicate, what is negotiated linguistically is filtered through what the participants believe about the world, what values they consider important for giving their society order and harmony, whether their culture values the individual or the group, whether the culture is oriented toward the future, present or past, what the society's goals are to justify its existence, and finally, what constitutes acceptable behaviors. These variables, vital for a culture's existence, are learned from birth. They form part of who one is. They put hue and tone to one's experiences.

Think of it this way. When you were a child, and your mother and/or father took you for walks in your stroller, and a friend or acquaintance or total stranger came up and started complimenting you on how beautiful you were, it is quite likely that your mother and/or father said something like this: "Say thank you!" Now you, being of a very young age, were not capable of saying anything save the interesting sounds that you would frequently babble. What your parents were doing was modeling the appropriate linguistic response for that particular situation. So that when, later in life, someone compliments you on your new hairstyle or new outfit or new car, you know automatically that the appropriate response to that situation is to say, "Thank you," and maybe go on about how the outfit was a little something you just picked up, or the new sports car is capable of generating 240 horsepower with a four-cylinder engine. Now, what is interesting is that the "thank you" your parents modeled for you, and which you eventually picked up, reflects a cultural value. This expression of gratitude is important to keep peace and harmony in a community where politeness is viewed as appropriate behavior. There are a myriad of these kinds of real-world cultural examples, as numerous as there are cultures. They are known by heart because they have been handed down in these carefully crafted "modeling" sessions known as human experience.

Sociocultural Variables

Socioculture has to do with group memberships that are important for shaping identity and behavior and the various roles played in those relationships. Admittedly, group membership is a broad topic which would take an immense time to cover, but for this book's purposes, it is sufficient to say that, while these identities take many forms, one's social groups include those sought for guidance in determining one's behavior (called "Reference Groups" by Gudykunst and Kim). These could be family units, church groups, civic clubs, whatever group in part shapes who one is and how one reacts to the world.

Included in this notion of group memberships is a topic which is rarely discussed but appears to be an intrinsic part of how societies structure themselves, the perception of in-group and out-group membership. Social identity, who one is in reference to the world in which one lives, certainly influences the groups one joins. Likewise, the groups of which one elects to become a member, and groups of which one is a member by virtue of birthplace, ethnicity and gender, determine whether or not one is viewed as being a member of an in-group or an out-group. In-groups and out-groups are variable depending upon who is doing the deciding, and they change over time. Today's in-group is yesterday's out-group. Certain publications are famous for telling people what is hot and what is not, what is in and what is out. For example, owning a schnauzer, eating pistachio-raisin frozen custard, and wearing cut-off jeans on dress-down Fridays is now in. Owning a chocolate Lab, eating chocolate ice cream, and wearing chocolate-colored "sans-a-belts" is out, at least for this year.

A second sociocultural feature is role relationships. This category includes not only the many roles played in life, but also issues like occupational prestige, cross-cultural differences in role relationships, the degree to which roles encourage or discourage personalness, the degree to which roles demand formality in manner and speech, the degree to which roles are hierarchical (perhaps the more prestigious the role, the higher the position in the social/political/economic hierarchy), and, finally, the degree of freedom given to deviate from life roles.

Psychocultural Variables

Categorization, stereotypes and attitudes characterize this important variable in communication. To make the world manageable, the ability to characterize and categorize it is needed. In doing so, one can, with varying degrees of accuracy, predict behavior to the extent that one "knows" when a situation is safe or dangerous, when a person is a friend or foe. Categorization further enables a person to relate one event to another.

Some categories of people and events are based on a multitude of experience. Some are based on a few random examples which serve to define the entire category. When a group is categorized on the basis of the behavior of a few members of that group, stereotypes arise. Stereotypes can be said to be both useful and dangerous; useful by virtue of the fact that they help create categories so that sense can be made of the world; dangerous because they can generate destructive behavior toward the stereotyped group. Stereotypes lead to attitudes which are interpretations of behavior of persons associated with a particular group. While, again, attitudes help make sense of the world and potentially protect people against enemies (real and perceived), they are often in error because people are multidimensional and perceive behavior differently. Moreover, a person's behavior cannot often be easily categorized. If stereotypes often lead to positive and/or negative attitudes toward groups, attitudes, especially negative ones, can lead to another important psychocultural variable, ethnocentrism, the view that one's own group is center of universe.

These psychocultural variables are important in the manner they influence communication. For example, say one of the reference groups of which you are an active member, the "Brown Eyes," possesses a number of negative stereotypes of green-eyed people. Suppose that these stereotypes have arisen based on the observed behaviors of a very few green-eyed people they are not particularly representative of green-eyed people, but enough members of the Brown Eyes have observed these same few Green Eyes to confirm their stereotypes. Further, suppose that the Brown Eyes have developed such negative attitudes toward green-eyed people that when they encounter green-eyed persons on the street, they call them terrible names, or avoid them altogether. What is more, when a green-eyed person applies for a position at one of the local businesses, he is assigned to a menial job and is rarely awarded promotions. The Green Eyes are subject to prejudice and discrimination to the extent that many have moved away from the area where the Brown Eyes live.

Environmental Variables

Communication is influenced by not only the physical environment in which it takes place, but by the psychological environment in which communication occurs. It is well-established that geography, climate, architecture and landscape shape communication. One recognized example of the influence of climate on human interaction is the fact that during hot summer months incidences of violent crime increase proportionately to the increase in temperature. Climate only tells part of the story. How members of a speech community view "time," whether a person compartmentalizes life (doing one thing at a time) or is able to balance several activities at once, affects how people communicate with each other. In the Appalachian region of North Carolina, people seem to be in both a monochronic (doing one thing at a time) and a polychronic (doing several things at once) world. For example, suppose a person wanted to transact some business with another; he would like to look at a car someone is selling. He would come to where the car is located, and the two might chat for maybe 20 or 30 minutes about all manners of things, usually starting with the weather (which in the mountains of North Carolina is either very good or very bad). They would close their chat with how the Carolina Panthers or one of the ACC college basketball teams is doing (in those parts it is usually North Carolina, but there are Wake, Duke and State fans around). All the while, not only is the person looking the car over, he is peppering the conversation with questions about mileage, rust, horsepower, maintenance, etc. So while looking over a car might commonly take 30 minutes (minus any test driving that is done), in that region the event may last for an hour, or even two if they know each other.

Negotiated Perspective

The case continues to build that grammatical choice is directly and intimately influenced by context, not only the specific context of the linguistic act, but the larger context of culture, broadly defined earlier. To reiterate and build upon this book's definition of grammar, grammar is the discoursal scaffold (the superstructure) by which a person is able to express and negotiate hybridized perspectives and co-create meaning with another person within a particular speech community. To put this another way, grammatical choice and use in communicative contexts is a matter of Negotiated Perspective, a designation this book uses to define the process which is intimately rooted in the process of human communication within definable cultural contexts.

It works like this. When one person engages another in conversation, he or she is constantly enabling the other to understand the picture in his or her mind. For example, I want you to see/understand an event the same way I do, and you want me to see /understand the event the same way you do. Therefore, I will construct a discourse which will highlight various concepts/themes/persons. I will strategically place these concepts/themes/persons in the structure of the discourse so that my picture of reality can be understood by you, the other participant in the conversation, or at least I hope it can. And so, discourse is constructed, grammatical structure imposed on it so that it will have meaning to the interlocutor. At least, that's the theory.

But the difficulty lies in the fact that the assumptions used to co-construct meaning in communication differ from context to context and from person to person. That is a complicated way of saying that people understand different things from the events they experience and the information they receive, even if they experience the event or receive the information together. Even if two or more people have witnessed the same event or are privy to the same information, and want to share the event or information with each other, they will invariably approach the communication with different experiences and a different understanding of the context. Therefore, they will have a completely different understanding of the sequence of the event, the importance, or lack thereof, of incidences within the event, and the importance, or lack thereof, of the information given them, etc.

So, for example, one interlocutor may come away from experiencing an event with one perspective, borne of his or her own knowledge of the world and his or her own experience, while another interlocutor may understand an event differently, borne of a knowledge of the world and experience which overlap to the extent that the two interlocutors understand each other, but are different enough that, at times, they may miscommunicate. How is it that we understand each other at all? How is it that we are able to communicate? Since language, and specifically grammatical form, is the means by which perspective is co-constructed or negotiated, and since perspectives may indeed be different, it stands to reason there is a certain unpredictability in communication. That unpredictability makes for very interesting relationships between spouses, friends, coworkers, and governments.

Negotiated Perspective is the key that unlocks the mystery of communication (illustrated in Figure 1). When entering into a conversation with each other, people ask a number of questions to themselves. Among the most important questions asked are: What does the speaker believe about herself? What does the speaker believe about the listener? What does the listener believe about the speaker? What does the listener believe about herself? What do the speaker and listener believe about the event? These questions are considered at such speed that people are unaware of asking them or even answering them. Moreover, these questions are ongoing during the entire course of the conversation. The discourse which results, including the myriad of grammatical forms which scaffold the discourse, is like a intricate tapestry, the whole picture comprising the shades and hues woven by each individual perspective.

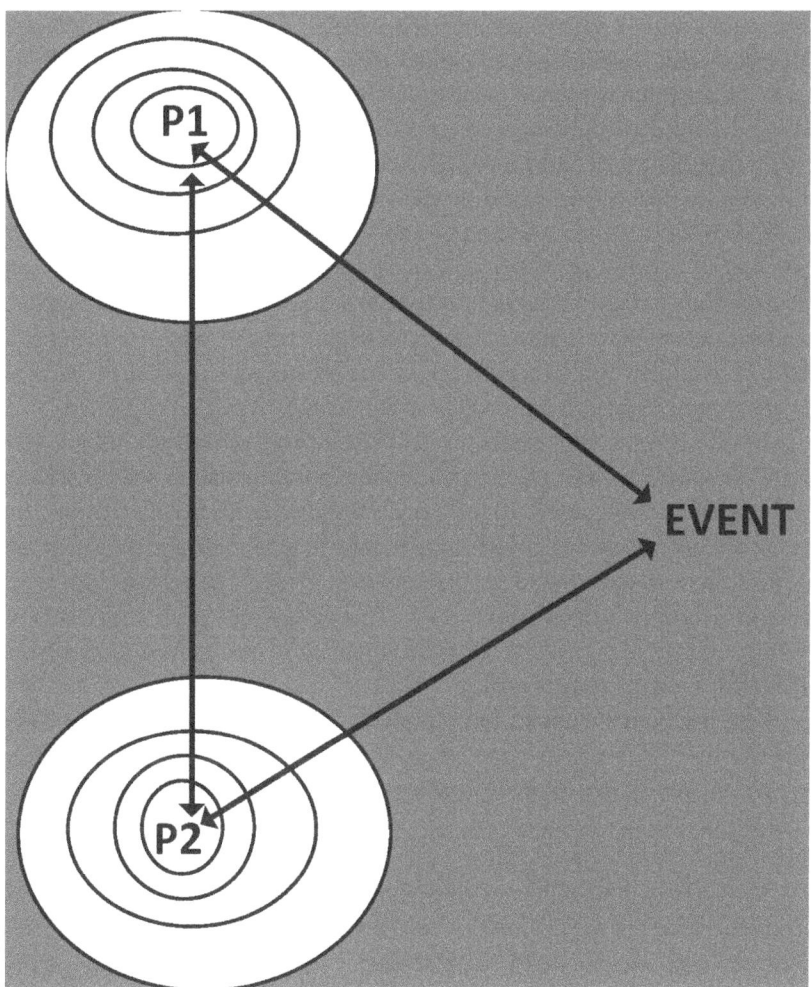

Figure 1: Negotiated Perspective. P1 and P2 represent participants in a conversation. The semi-concentric circles represent various filters through which communication happens (e.g., one's understanding of culture, one's role in society, one's personality, etc.). These filters are non-concentric to represent the high degree of variability in a person's perspective and experience.

To use another metaphor, the negotiation of perspective in discourse is like the elaborate interweaving of a symphonic piece, each discrete (and often different) theme blending with the next, and the next, etc. Educator Marrion Ward views the notion of Negotiated Perspective as a process in three "movements": movement toward coordination, movement toward cooperation, and movement toward collective communication.[10] These movements are not meant to be viewed as being disconnected, but rather as a simultaneous symphony where all parts are played mostly synchronously.

The movement toward coordination comprises the initiation of discourse, wherein participants enter the discourse with their own experience and knowledge of the world, and their individual perspectives on the particular situation being discussed. In this initial movement, participants establish their roles in the conversation (who speaks when, whose story is heard first, when to interrupt, etc.). Likewise, participants elicit the necessary information needed to understand the stories being told (asking questions for clarification, information, sharing background information, etc.). It is in this movement that each participant is interpreting the event in terms of her own experience and knowledge of the world.

In the second movement of this discoursal symphony, movement toward cooperation, participants coordinate their schemas (their background knowledge and experience, all interlaced in these complex neural networks, discussed earlier) toward a shared understanding of the information or the event. This is accomplished by questioning, clarifying, backsliding, what Professor Ward calls "discoordination" ("No! That's not at all what I meant. I meant…"), reaffirmation, or what this book calls "recoordination," and, if successful, mutual understanding.

The final movement of the symphony is like the "being on the same page of music" movement. It is where the participants in the conversation develop and affirm new ways of working together, constructing a new understanding of the world based on the negotiation of their distinct perspectives.

Here are two examples to show how this works. The first example is typical of how the same situation is interpreted differently. Suppose that there was a minor car accident yesterday. The local news reported it this way: "Two cars collided but no one was seriously injured, although there was serious damage to both cars. It was reported that one of the drivers, Paul Smith of Millville, ran a red light and collided with a car driven by Julia Gomez of Baytown."

Suppose that you know both Paul and Julia, and that you had heard of the accident on the news. At a restaurant the day after the accident, you run into (not literally) a friend of yours who happens to be a good friend of Paul. Further, this mutual friend of Paul does not know Julia. In the midst of your conversation, Paul's accident comes up. Your friend says, "Did you know that Paul was involved in an accident yesterday? He was driving through the intersection of Water and Rivers St. and unfortunately didn't notice the light had turned red. He ran into another car but, thank goodness, he was not hurt. You know he has been under a lot of stress lately breaking up with his girlfriend and all. It's sad! He just bought that car."

Later that day, you run into (again, not literally) another friend at the office. This friend knows Julia well but does not know Paul at all. The conversation turns to the accident, and your friend says, "Did you hear that Julia was in an accident yesterday? She was driving along minding her own business when some idiot not paying attention to what he was doing ran a red light and plowed into her. Fortunately, she wasn't hurt, but she was sure mad. I don't blame her. I would have been mad too."

Consider now how perspective is used to construct each friend's discourse. The friend of Paul relates the event to circumstances she has had with or that she knows about Paul. Moreover, the friend relates commonly-held experiences (the accident, Paul's breakup with his girlfriend and the fact that Paul's wrecked car was new), or at least relates these experiences out of the assumption that you know about them, as realized by the "you know" statements in the discourse. The focus is clearly on Paul in this discourse. The other driver, Julia in this case, is not mentioned at all.

The recast of the story from Julia's friend is similar to that of Paul's friend. Julia is clearly the focus of the narrative by virtue of the fact that she is mentioned repeatedly. Paul is mentioned in Julia's friend's discourse, but not by name. Further, the mentions are overtly negative. Paul is portrayed as "some idiot" who was inattentive to his driving and who "plowed" into her car, plowing seemingly carrying more negative weight than "running into" or even "crashing."

These three narratives, including the report of the accident in the local paper, are indicative of how Negotiated Perspective works. Each teller of the tale views the tale from his or her own unique viewpoint. Furthermore, each teller of the tale wants the hearer to "see" the event from this viewpoint, i.e., wants the hearer to have the same picture in her head as the teller. (At the end of this chapter in the Now You Try It! section, there is an opportunity to discover what might happen if Paul's friend and Julia's friend got together for a chat about the accident.)

The second example is more specific and culturally-based. Consider the well-used expression of leave-taking in Appalachian English, "Let's go to the house." Grammatically, the phrase is in the form of a cohortative, a polite first-person command form often used in invitations such as "Let's go to lunch," or "Let's dance." However, the person using the phrase has no intention of inviting the person with whom she is talking to go home with her. If the speaker wanted to extend an invitation, she would probably use something like, "Won't you come over for a while?" or "Come on over for supper." To fully understand the meaning of the phrase, "Let's go to the house," the hearer would have to understand something about the Appalachian culture. In Appalachia, a premium is placed upon the value of relationships, especially with family members and close friends. Language usage reflects that value. When someone says to you, "Let's go to the house," he or she is, in effect, saying that the relationship shared between you is important, but that it is time to leave: "I will go to my house and you will go to yours." But when you meet again, that relationship will be on the same strong footing as before. So, the cohortative in this instance is simply a way for an Appalachian person to say "goodbye," but it "means" that the persons who are participating in the conversation are all included in the leave-taking and in a common community. While the grammar carries the message, one has to use one's understanding of the particular culture in which the language event happened to understand the message.

THE FOUR PERSPECTIVES

Negotiated Perspective is a useful metaphor for describing the role of grammar in communication. Negotiated Perspective further comprises four interconnected components under which most all if not all grammatical function in English can be subsumed.

Perspective of Time and Space

The first of these components is the Perspective of Time and Space. Language is extremely functional because it allows human beings to tell stories. Creating narrative is one of the characteristics of the human brain that makes human beings unique among creatures. Linguists such as Mark Turner and George Lakoff continue to formulate hypotheses about the role narrative plays in the development of language and learning.[11] As demonstrated in a following chapter about prepositions, Turner's theory of Narrative Imaging hinges on the notion that humans construct narrative, small stories that are projected onto and into each other. The projections of small stories are the building blocks of complex neurological schema from whence people categorize their experiences in the world and learn new things. Two of the basic elements of narrative consist of events/actions in time and space. Time and space encompass when and where an event (an action or state) is happening. Time perspective can be in the past, in present time, or in the future (the potentiality of action).

The Perspective of Time and Space, encompassing the notion of linear events (one event after another in sequence and time), is manifest grammatically in such overt components as prepositions, adverbs and, perhaps its most important example, the verb. As far as the verb is concerned, all verbs carry at least some facet of time, even some modals which represent "time as potential."

Perspective of Condition

Second, the Perspective of Condition embodies how an event is happening or not happening. Condition encompasses such traditional grammatical notions as aspect (whether an action is lasting over a longer period of time or lasting over a shorter period of time), whether an action is transitive (an actor doing something to someone else), degree of completion (perfect vs. imperfect), stative, and modality — in other words, action, state and potential.

To illustrate the Perspective of Condition, take transitive verbs as an example. To review what you no doubt learned back in your grammar class (whether it was in the eighth grade or an ESL/EFL class), a transitive verb is one that takes an object, usually defined as an action verb where an agent initiates an action on something or someone. "John kissed Mary" is an example of this type of verb. Think of it in terms of the widespread television show *Cops*. By far, the most popular pieces of the program are scenes in which the police chase a criminal at high speed, and when they catch him (it's usually a him), they arrest him in this high-stakes drama that usually involves running, guns, more running, shouting, more running, handcuffs and the ground. What we see through the lens of the video camera is this action taking place. Agents carrying out actions, undergoers undergoing the action of the agents. And it rivets us. We like action. Think about if the directors of *Cops* decided, instead of showing police chases, they would station a police car on the side of the road, and show road scenes while the officer wrote her reports. Or if there was an entire television channel dedicated to showing continuous coverage of one of the DOT (Department of Transportation) cameras on the side of an interstate highway.

Perspective of Focus

The third component of perspective is the Perspective of Focus. The Perspective of Focus is important in the discussion of English grammar because it embodies a very essential discoursal concept, point of view, termed in the linguistic world, Empathy. The term Empathy, as a linguistic hypothesis, was first coined by Susumu Kuno, who proposed what he called a hierarchy of empathy, which is a representation of the speaker's attitude toward the other participants, which can be people or things, in an event.

Think of it this way. Suppose you are on vacation in Paris, and you are visiting the Eiffel Tower. You have always wanted to see the Eiffel Tower, and standing on the terrace at the Palais de Chaillot, you are awed by the marvelous sight, the Eiffel Tower before you framed by the marvelous fountains of the Palais de Chaillot. So you pull out your new digital camera for a picture. Now, since you have always wanted to see the Eiffel Tower, and since it *is* truly breathtaking, you would probably want to put it in the center of the picture.

Empathy can be likened to camera angles, specifically where a speaker will choose to focus a certain participant or theme in one instance and another in a different context. Professor Kuno, in a study he co-authored with a fellow linguist, Professor Kaburaki, gives the following examples to illustrate the concept of empathy:

> John kissed Mary.
> John kissed his wife.
> Mary's husband kissed her.
> Mary was kissed by John.[12]

In the first example, the imaginary photographer chooses a family portrait (a romantic family portrait — Kuno's "hit" is changed to "kiss") including both John and Mary and the centerpiece of the event, their smooch. According to Kuno, the speaker chooses to report the event objectively, that is, the camera is placed at an appropriate distance from both John and Mary so that the imaginary photographer can center both in the picture. Without the context to further say who is more in focus, neither participant is in more obvious focus than the other. That is, John has been caught on camera in the act of kissing Mary, but one does not know if Mary egged him on to do it or if John is simply wanting to show his unprompted affection.

In the second photograph, John is in the center of the picture, in closer focus, due to the fact that he is mentioned by name, and the reference to Mary is made in terms of John. Think of it this way. Someone looking at the picture may ask, "Who is that woman John's kissing?" "Oh, that's his wife," you reply. A possible retort to, "Oh that's his wife," might be, "Hmm, I didn't know John was married." In other words, John is immediately recognizable in the photo because the questioner knows him and not the object of his affection in the picture.

The focus is reversed in the third photograph, Mary's husband kissed her. The photographer has chosen to put Mary into sharper focus by referring to her by name as the possessor of a husband, who remains unnamed. "Hey, look here, Mary's husband, I forget his name now, I've only met him a couple times, kissed her." "John" is viewed in light of Mary.

Finally, in the last photo, the camera is placed closer to Mary than John. In fact, through the use of the passive, one could, if one had particular antipathy toward John, leave him out of the picture altogether. So, it is not necessary to say Mary was kissed by John. One can just leave him out of the picture.

Perspective of Interaction

Finally, the Perspective of Interaction embodies one of the key elements for understanding how language works, relationships, harking back to the discussion earlier in this book. Human communication is built around assumptions: assumptions people make about each other, and assumptions people make about the event or events about which they are talking. The expression of these relationships is embodied in almost every component of language, especially verbal characteristics such aspect (condition), voice (passive vs. active), mood (subjunctive vs. indicative), and modality. Relationships in a great sense determine how those communicating which each other "view" and "negotiate" an action, state or action potential. Given this, later there will be discussion of three interesting "speech acts," manipulatives (namely negatives), interrogatives and imperatives. Perspective and meaning are established in terms of the degree to which the interlocutors wish to change the status quo. The degree to which that change is actually carried out is predicated on the relationship between the ones communicating.

MOTIVATIONAL VALENCE

So far, it has been demonstrated that one's perspective as negotiated in discourse allows speakers to understand each other and communication to take place. But how do speakers decide what is important and not important in an event?

This book refers to this process as Motivational Valence. Motivational Valence, a term suggested by Peter Kalivas, a leading neuroscientist at the Medical University of South Carolina, can be defined as "the potential that one's perspective will be attracted toward or repulsed away from an event."[13] As perspective is gradable, so is Motivational Valence. One can be strongly, moderately or mildly attracted or repulsed. In any case, the level of attraction or repulsion will determine how engaged one will be to an event. Now, this may seem self-evident, but the importance of Motivational Valence lies in how it effects grammar.

At the very end of one of my grammar classes a few years back, a class on gerunds and infinitives, one of the brightest students I have ever been privileged to teach asked the following question.

"What about, 'I shudder to think'? Isn't that highly emotionally charged?"

Although I didn't have time to give him anything but a somewhat rambling, end-of-class kind of answer, the more I thought about his question, the more I realized he had given me an unbelievable gift, a jewel that wonderfully illustrates how Motivational Valence works, and that he fully understood how it works.

Look at it this way. The higher the degree of Motivational Valence, the higher the attraction toward an event, the more likely a speaker will use a gerund. Conversely, the lower the degree of motivational valence, the higher the repulsion away from the event, the more likely the speaker will use an infinitive. Why use an infinitive with the verb, "to shudder," a verb with a high degree of emotion (and one would think a higher level of attraction to the event). But actually, "I shudder to think" signifies a momentary emotional response leading to feelings of revulsion or distaste. While the verb carries high emotion, it creates low Motivational Valence in that there is no motivation to consider the event that caused the "shuddering." Therefore, the infinitive following "shudder" reflects low Motivational Valence. More will be said about this later in Chapter 6.

THE MASCAGNI EFFECT REVISITED

One sunny morning in late summer, while strolling with my friend Bill Wilson, discussing things language and music, I happened to ask him what he was teaching in his music appreciation class that afternoon.[14]

"The Intermezzo to *Cavalleria Rusticana* by Mascagni," he replied.

"Wow, what a beautiful piece. It is one of the most sensual and romantic pieces I have ever heard," I said, to which he furrowed his brow and looked at me with a "What planet are you from?" look.

"Romantic? I cry every time I hear that piece. Tragic! Purely tragic.

Nothing particularly sensual about it. Not a piece I would put on the CD player in my sports car on a hot date."

I was perplexed. How could we have such different views of the same piece of music? Now, we were both familiar with the piece, he more so than me. I had heard it several times listening to the radio. He had heard it countless times while viewing *Cavalleria Rusticana*.

Not long after I had this discussion with Bill Wilson, I happened to be channel surfing, and landed on the last 15 or so minutes of the movie *Godfather III*. In the scene, seemingly the entire cast was shot, hanged, poisoned, or summarily garroted. In the last scene of the trilogy, as the Corleone family descended the steps of an Italian opera house somewhere, probably Sicily, an assassin dressed as a priest pulled a gun and shot into the family, hitting the daughter of Don Michael Corleone in the heart. She died a tragic death on the Scala (steps), Michael wailing inconsolably. In a scene which was both touching and heart-wrenching, the mother of the slain daughter cradled the girl in her arms as the intermezzo to *Cavalleria Rusticana* played mournfully in the background. It was then I understood what my colleague, Bill Wilson, was saying to me about the intermezzo to *Cavalleria Rusticana*, because, I too, experienced a bit of what he experienced.

The process in which I began to understand the perspective of my friend is what occurs daily in communication. This is the Mascagni Effect. And while Mascagni himself, or *Cavalleria Rusticana* for that matter, has little to do with the effect named in his honor, the process whereby one interlocutor understands the perspective of another is crucial for effective communication in any context.

As speakers negotiate meaning by enabling their hearers to understand their perspectives, grammatical choice depends greatly upon the situation and how the speaker and listener perceives it. Often subtle pragmatic factors, which will be covered throughout this text, influence people choosing one grammatical form over another. People rarely make time-consuming decisions about them, although sometimes the decision to use one form over another is quite conscious. The process of making the decision to use one grammatical form over another is so refined, efficient and instantaneous as to seem automatic and unconscious. How these pragmatic factors interact with grammatical form is the subject of the discussions of the following chapters, each covering a particular "question of why." It is hoped that, by asking these "questions of why," teachers, future teachers and students will be enabled to reach the proverbial fork in the road in order that they might understand, and in some sense, create a new reality based on the Negotiated Perspective of discourse.

From Personal Experience: Negotiated Perspective and Language Learning

Background

As important as it is to posit a theory of grammar, it is equally important to test the theory through rigorous observation and experiential analysis. In order determine the reliability and validity of the theory conceived in this text, a conglomeration of integrated components called the Mascagni Effect, I decided to put myself into the role of language learner in a host culture where the language is utilized by native speakers for everyday communication. The language of choice was French, and the culture, the Pays de la Loire in western France, more specifically, the city of Angers. I had studied French in junior high and in high school, having lived in the southern French city of Narbonne during the summer of my junior year. Except for one course in college, I had not formally studied the language until I arrived in Angers, and even then, I was not enrolled in a formal course of study, deciding rather to immerse myself into the world of conversation.

As discussed earlier, language is best acquired when the link between context and what the learner expects will happen linguistically within that context is effortless. The unexpected, the disconnect between what one expects to happen linguistically and what actually happens, is what creates the roadblocks between successful communication and that which goes awry.

To illustrate this point, consider the context of purchasing goods and services in a store and the linguistic expectations of the encounter. Buying items involves certain physical activity which spans culture, and are thus said to be "scripted." Moreover, transactions require language which, while the actual language spoken is different, the linguistic script is similar across cultures, familiar enough for strangers in the host culture to be able to purchase items successfully. So, "*Trente-sept euro et cinquante centimes, s'il vous plait*" is pretty much the same script as "that will be thirty-seven fifty, please," the exchange rate between the euro and U.S. dollar notwithstanding.

The script runs as follows. The buyer selects items for purchase, approaches the cashier, and either gives the items to the cashier or places them on a conveyor. The cashier scans or punches in the price of the item, relates this price to the customer, who may or may not understand the amount. The buyer proffers money in some amount to the cashier, who may or may not return change to the customer depending upon a couple of factors like whether the customer has the correct amount, and whether the customer has understood both the cashier's statement and the currency, in which case the customer may give the cashier the largest bill possible and receive change. Following the exchange of money, the cashier or a bagger places the item in a bag, thanks the customer, and the transaction ends.

However, even though this script is common if the customer and the cashier transact business in a typical store in the United States, there are still variations on this theme, depending upon what is purchased where. In a grocery store, for example, the cashier or the bagger may ask whether the customer would prefer a plastic bag or a paper bag. The common scripted question goes something like, "Paper or plastic?", or "Is plastic okay?", if that is the most accessible bag available.

Depending upon which region of the United States the transaction takes place, the customer and cashier might engage in a short conversation before or during the transaction. In the South, this scenario is more common generally than in other regions, since it considered culturally rude not to acknowledge the other's presence, and to at least make a cursory inquiry about the person's general state of health, even if the two do not know each other. In more rural areas of the U.S., depending upon how many shoppers are in the checkout line, the conversation may be protracted. But what commonly occurs in one culture may be quite unexpected for strangers from other or foreign cultures. For example, in Turkey, it is customary to join the salesperson in several rounds of tea during the transaction. Often, tea is served when the customer is seriously considering an item, when negotiations occur, and when an agreement on the price is made and the parties to the agreement shake hands.

In France, it has been my personal experience that the script of purchasing items from stores large and small, even from vendors in the outdoor markets, is quite similar to that in the United States, with two notable exceptions; linguistic exceptions, to be precise, that arose in the form of two unexpected questions: 1. Would you like a bag for your items?, and 2. The more unexpected, Where do you live? In the United States, there are retailers which gather demographic data for marketing purposes. To wit, clerks may ask for a shopper's zip code at check out. But the latter question occurs with such regularity that it forms a part of the usual script.

What makes this hurdle formidable is not the difficulty of the questions themselves, but rather, it may be one of a myriad of unexpected obstacles that crop up in the course of a day. Fortunately, these scripts are somewhat established and predictable and, because of their ubiquity, easily learnable, if the learner has enough experience with them to recognize their predictability. But, after multiple experiences in different contexts, the script becomes eventually entrenched within the learner's long-term memory, and thus, second-nature. The appropriate metaphor for this process may well be the actor or actress on stage with a particular role to play. Lines are learned, staging perfected, the script played out day upon day, week upon week *ad infinitem*.

Of course, the more difficult hurdles of language acquisition require significantly more time and experience to clear. These consist of those linguistic events which either radically defy an expected script, or those for which there is no script at all to impart meaning. Unfortunately, the most difficult discourse is often the most widespread, i.e., everyday conversation whose course is determined by the interlocutors. Among the greatest difficulties facing a language learner, certainly one of the most difficult for me, is how to process seemingly incessant input from multiple sources. More specifically, how does one determine what information is foregrounded, that is, information that requires some focus, and what is backgrounded, that is, what one can simply ignore?

Upon arrival into the host culture, one is suddenly struck by the sheer quantity of the second language being used, language which is not only spoken, but also found in printed form. Moreover, one is struck by how much language in the air is unrecognizable. Conversations between native speakers occur at a seemingly staccato pace. Questions are asked with little waste of time and effort, responses expected with the same fluency and immediacy. Immersion into a host culture can be an overwhelming experience, despite semesters spent in L2 classrooms acquiring the necessary "language background," essential vocabulary and grammar, to form coherent discourse in the host culture.

The first days in the host culture both excite the learner and terrify him or her. Almost everything feels and looks new even if the learner is similar with the host culture, and even if the host culture is somewhat analogous with the native culture; even if, as was my case, the learner had visited the host culture on occasion. The terror arises when the learner is forced to speak, which, in the context of the host culture, is inevitable. "Terror," in this case, is not akin to the sense one gets when watching a Stephen King film, for example. Rather, the learner finds him or herself lacking control of situations which are ordinarily easily manipulated, the often tremendous sense of discomfort at having limited capacity to communicate ideas, feelings, etc., that one desires to communicate in order to negotiate the necessities of life in a new language and in a new place. In other words, the stranger may feel him or herself isolated in the host culture. The difficulty lies in the fact that, though the learner is immersed in the host culture, the cacophony does not suddenly become lucid, at least in the first month or two. In fact, in my experience, the acquisition of language may be decelerated by what I call *l'embrouillement de la langue*, the language jumble.

This jumble is caused by three factors, mostly environmental in nature, or, at least, contextual. These three are:

1. The absolute and incontrovertible need to communicate within the host culture.
2. The enormous amount of input from a variety of sources within the host culture, and the brain's learned efficiency for processing it.
3. The attempt to reconcile often systematic and binary literacy-based learning strategies in the L2 classroom with common-usage strategies, which are, for the most part, non-binary and asystematic.

These three factors are the most formidable hurdles in language acquisition. And given this dynamic, two essential questions must be raised, namely: 1. How does the learner, whose acquisitional experience consists of building an L2 which is highly scripted, predictable, and time-insensitive, become responsive to language which is multinary, time-sensitive and often highly unpredictable?; and 2. A corollary of the first question, What enabling strategies are available to the learner, immersed in the host culture, that accentuate not only language but cultural acquisition?

The Need to Communicate

Of the various factors influencing the acquisition of a second language, the realization that there is an indisputable need to communicate may the single most important one. Perhaps it can be said that this overwhelming need to communicate in the many contexts of the host culture not only occasions this language jumble, it heightens it.

To illustrate this point, consider the complexity of negotiating everyday life; consider the many contexts that are present during the course of a single day, contexts each comprising their own linguistic discourses. From the earliest age, native speakers are exposed to a myriad of contexts, each with its inherent discourses, both verbal and non-verbal. Through the process of repetition, these contexts become entrenched, and form the basis of one's ability to negotiate new contexts with some ease. Experience and the instantiation of perspective are the key factors that enable speakers to gain automaticity in their native languages and cultures.

These cultural complexities exist everywhere and in all cultures. For the stranger, the communicative demands inherent in the host culture often exist as roadblocks to learning. Put another way, it is rarely the extraordinary that trips learners of a second language. Rather, it is the small, seemingly unimportant events that, through a lack of familiarity on the part of the learner, appear unexpectedly, and cause difficulties.

For example, applying for a bank account in my native culture and in my native language, the USA and English in this case, is a relatively simple process of completing an application, followed by depositing an appropriate amount of money into the new account. The person opening the account is given a temporary debit card to use until the permanent card arrives in the mail, usually in the course of a week or two. There are, of course, a host of account options from which to choose, and the sheer number of options as well as the particular language used in the context of opening an account may be quite confusing to a learner of English in the United States, especially if it in any way deviates from the process to which the learner is accustomed.

In France, the process, while not extraordinarily difficult, does have enough inherent differences to cause some confusion, especially for strangers like me with some familiarity with the language and the culture. In France, one applies, signs what seems to be a ream of official documents, and then waits a day before depositing any money, or until the paperwork has made its way through the system. As in the United States, at the same time one opens an account, one applies for a debit card. But unlike the U.S., the applicant must physically go to the bank where the application is made and pick up the card. I had not understood this, and so I waited and waited for the card to come in the mail. When I inquired at the bank, they told me that the card was here, and asked hadn't I received a letter to that effect. I simply smiled, and thought to myself, "Oh, that's what that letter said." As a addendum to this story, once one collects his or her bank card, making transactions of any kind in France becomes quite simple and seamless.

Another context with its implicit roadblocks is obtaining the necessary *Carte de Séjour* to live and work in France. This necessary identity card must be in one's possession at all times, especially if one has designs on leaving the country and being able to return. Problems can occur in any number of places up and down the line of the cumbersome French bureaucracy, and can be especially tricky if the sponsoring agency makes an error, so that the stranger needs not only to obtain the *Carte de Séjour* but also to amend his or her visa in the process. In this case, the stranger gets shifted from one office to another, greeted with both politeness and respect, and, in the end, gets either a shrug of the shoulder meaning, "It's not our fault that they screwed up," or a smile and a "We'll take a look at it." Amazingly, despite what seems to be a ridiculously unwieldy system of red tape, civil servants in France are dedicated to their jobs and, for the most part, do not give tasks the short shrift.

What causes the confusion, in this case, is that the French social system is built upon a strict Cartesian philosophy which is centuries old. The Cartesian world, as suggested above in the discussion of Chomsky, is binary, operating in the sharp contrasts of black and white. There are no shades of gray in this conception of the world. To use an analogy, if what you possess is black, and you need white, the Cartesian mind cannot comprehend this. It is black because it is black, and there are complex processes in place that ensure that if you need black, you will most assuredly get black. In such a system, you get black even if you need white.

For many Americans who do not operate in such a binary frame of reference, this world view is nonsensical. If one errs by giving someone something black when he or she really wanted white, one commonly admits the error, or passes the error down the line so as to cover one's back to avoid legal action. If the stranger has black and needs white, and if the stranger received black through no fault of his or her own, functionaries will usually go out of their way to exchange black for white, or if white is not available; exchange it for a nice shade of gray which works just as well.

In the quotidian life in a host culture, turbulence roils everywhere, from trying to explain to a stylist how one wants his or her hair cut, to responding to direct questions at a dinner party when one is not sure what the topic of conversation is. The unexpected in the expected is the problem, the misunderstanding or non-understanding of context, and therefore, the inability to construct/co-construct meaningful discourse, thereby hindering the process of negotiated perspective. However, if, as we have seen, the unexpected holds the ingredients of the jumble of language, it is also, curiously, the embrouillement's cure.

L'Embrouillement de la Langue: *The Language Jumble*

The second point is crucial to our understanding how negotiated perspective and second language acquisition coalesce. The theory here is that the learner's ability or inability to discern what is important in the nearly immeasurable quantity of input hinges, in large part, upon the learner's prior experience with the L2 and with the host culture. Learners with little or no experience in the second language expend little effort trying to understand extended discourse. They have either learned rudimentary, but necessary, phrases in the language to negotiate the culture, or they pick them up on site. Likewise, those fluent in the language, those who would be classified as having advanced proficiency, require a modicum of effort to discern foregrounded from backgrounded in the myriad of discourses they experience. By contrast, learners who possess some knowledge and experience with the language and the host culture, those assessed as having intermediate proficiency, are likely to experience a heightened sense of this "language jumble." At least that has been my experience in France.

A bit of background may be helpful in explaining this point. As a junior in high school I lived and studied French language and culture in the Languedocian town of Narbonne. Through this experience, I was able to greatly enhance what I had learned over three years of classroom instruction. I subsequently lost that ability over time due through disuse. Before my semester in France, I attempted to regain some proficiency through grammatical study, and by listening to French media. While I had made several previous visits to France before my arrival in January 2011, my ability to communicate in French, that is, the capacity to understand what was being conveyed to me as well as the capacity to respond appropriately, was indeed limited, even though the host culture, in this case, the France of Maine et La Loire, proved to be a good fit. I was comfortable in France even with an intermediate proficiency in the language. Over time, the linguistic clutter seemed to wax and wane, depending upon need and context.

My hypothesis is that the experience of the "Language Jumble" is neither isolated nor particularly uncommon. Rather, it is a product of the stranger's need to concentrate a significant amount of attention on both the discourse at hand and upon that which he or she has previously learned either through classroom or direct experience in the host culture. The learner must be able to listen intently, comprehend, and respond with some immediacy. Enduring this "stage" of language acquisition may well be the precursor to one's ability to speak and comprehend with increasing fluency and automaticity. I use the term "stage" loosely, however. The beginning and ending of this "embrouillement" is not so well defined, that is, one may possess an advanced level of proficiency, and still find him or herself in contexts which are baffling, contexts wherein he or she may become suddenly mute.

A question arises at this point: How does the brain attune to this input and adjust its neural processes to unscramble the jumble? Or to put it a bit differently, what strategies, both psychological and pedagogical, help the learner categorize this abundant amount of new information? And is age a factor? What is the influence of time, i.e., how much time does a learner need, especially one considered "older" (and I'll leave that definition to you the reader), to be able to comprehend, efficiently categorize, and achieve a high level of fluency and automaticity in the L2? These questions are difficult to make hard and fast generalizations for every learner in every context. It depends. Some learners have had significant practice learning languages, and have thus honed appropriate strategies for fluency. Others have not, or their strategies have grown rusty through disuse.

Motivation plays an important role in either heightening or easing this stage of linguistic confusion. Some learners are motivated to increase their level of fluency despite whatever setbacks or frustrations they may encounter along their journey. Others may have the opposite reaction and become less motivated to continue. Suffice it to say, however, that despite whatever language proficiency the learner has been able to accrue in the host culture, despite the learner's motivations, this stage of puzzlement is a normal stage in the process of language acquisition.

Little Defeats, Little Victories

Over time, the language jumble becomes less confusing due to the learner's increasing familiarity with the various contexts and discourses of everyday life. But what is required of the learner is an abundance of observation and risk-taking. In fact, I would go as far to say that this may well be the most important strategy a learner can carry in his or her methodological toolkit. For the learner to place him or herself intentionally into a context where the unexpected is likely to happen, to attempt to swim through the shifting currents of discourse, is important. In addition to observation and risk-taking, I would suggest two additional strategies to aid the second-language learner.

Practice Breeds Familiarity

It is said that practice makes perfect, and to a great extent that is likely the case. But not completely. There remain components of language that require years of practice and yet may still evade even the most capable learner. For native English speakers learning French, it is the gender system. In English, such a highly complex system that marks gender does not exist. English only marks nouns in terms of their specificity and importance (see Chapter 2 for an in-depth discussion of articles). The problem facing English speakers is that there is little or no correlation between the noun itself and the gender it possesses. For example, there is no one-to-one correspondence between the noun *lune* (moon) and its feminine gender. This is likewise the case with *soleil* (sun) and its assigned masculine gender. It is highly likely that native speakers of French acquired the noun and its gendered article together in various contexts and through years of experience and practice — of course, not the rote practice of the classroom.

Gender is not the only difficulty. Some grammatical/semantic systems are quite difficult to master. In common-usage language, speakers of French rarely use the entire range of the tense/aspect system, even though they probably could. In conversation, speakers generally use the present, passé compose (completed action in the past), the imperfect (ongoing past), and in certain contexts, the present form of the subjunctive (speakers of Spanish use it far more often).

For learners immersed in the French language in France, one very helpful strategy is to be highly perceptive; to discern the most common grammatical forms and use them. In other words, imitate what native speakers are doing. It is not helpful to spend a great deal of time memorizing verb forms in the imperfect subjunctive. You may find occasion to use such a form, but probably not!

Another helpful strategy for the learner to become familiar with the language is to find a conversational partner. After finding that I needed more opportunities to speak French with native speakers, I enrolled in a program called *Français en Action*, sponsored by the English Language Library of Angers. In this program, learners of French are paired with native speakers. The pair meets weekly or twice per week and converses for one hour in the L2. Conversations are typically informal, rich with common-usage vocabulary and phrases, as well as the inherent grammatical structures used in common-usage speech. The one-on-one learning environment enables the learner to build new information, new structures onto what he or she already knows. Moreover, these contextual discourses build the most important component of all, confidence. Perhaps the most enduring strategy for language learners, one that I often begin a semester with, is: "Learn without hesitation, speak without fear!"

Familiarity Breeds Familiarity

After almost three months of being immersed in French culture and language, not only had my familiarity with the scripts of everyday life increased, but my fluidity/fluency in the language had as well. What had been the most effective strategies? I would list three:

1. Lack of fear even when frustrated.
2. Intentionally placing myself within contexts where I am forced to use the language, even on days when I feel hesitant.
3. Increasing my familiarity with the *ésprit français*, the French mindset.

I have come to better understand those who speak this L2, their habits, their ways of thinking, their ways of relating to the world and to those around them. This understanding has enabled me to link language with speaker with context. The intersection of these three elements has allowed me to construct a French perspective which is, in many ways, integrated into my perspective as a native speaker of English from a particular English-speaking context, but, in many ways, is apart from that perspective as well. With time, and importantly, with experience, that perspective has been molded, negotiated, to the extent that I find myself slowly but perceptively growing bicultural.

Now You Try It!

Understanding the Role of Discourse

Discourse can be defined as a linguistic event in a particular context. The journey to understand the structure of the English language is predicated on a number of important questions: How is it that language-users interpret what other language-users intend to convey? How is it that people, as language-users, make sense of what speakers mean despite what they say, recognize connected, coherent discourse, and successfully take part in the complex activity called conversation? To answer these questions is to provide ourselves an appropriate context to assess the structure of English.

- Who were the participants (approximate age, gender, ethnicity)?
- Who initiated the conversation? Why was it initiated?
- What was the emotional tone of the conversation (friendly, serious, sarcastic, etc.)?
- Who spoke first? How was turn-taking established? Who spoke last?
- What kinds of gestures were used during the conversation? How would you describe the conversants' body language? Did they stand close to one another? Did they touch one another?
- Did anyone else enter into the conversation? What kinds of rules were observed for others entering the conversation?

What kind of language was used (formal, informal, slang)? If the conversants used slang, what specific words or phrases did they use which lead you to believe it was slang?

Understanding the Role of Negotiated Perspective

As defined in Chapter 1, Negotiated Perspective is the means by which the perspectives of the interlocutors in a communicative event are co-constructed using language, and specifically grammatical form. The goal of this activity is to discover how Negotiated Perspective operates in conversation. To accomplish this, one needs a story which involves events and characters. The task is to tell the story to several different people from several different perspectives. The process is as follows:

- Choose four or five people to listen to a story.
- Tell the story from the perspective of a particular character, changing the perspective each time you tell the story.
- Ask the hearer to recast/retell the story to you as he/she understood it.
- Ask the hearers to retell the story to each other.
- How were the stories similar?
- How were the stories different?

The Friends Meet

In one of the examples in Chapter 1, there was a story of Paul and Julia and their unfortunate traffic accident. One of Paul's friends and one of Julia's friends both happen to be friends of yours. Suppose you decide to test Negotiated Perspective by inviting both friends over for dinner to chat about the accident. So after dinner, you bring up the accident and watch while the friend's narratives intertwine (or unravel). What do you think will happen? Give a likely discourse as it unfolds and is negotiated. Remember, negotiating does not necessarily mean agreeing (negotiated perspective might mean the friends part, never speaking to one another again).

2
Articles: Julie and the French Sailor

THE QUESTION

Dating back to when I first started teaching English as a second language, the question of how to use the English article system has come up time and again. A few years ago, for example, a Chinese student lingered after class and asked: "**What is the difference between *a* and *the* and when do you know when to use one or the other?**" The question is intriguing because I had always assumed that English articles were among the least of grammatical problems for non-native speakers. It can be reasoned that they are simple words with simple meanings. Perhaps another reason to have not given much thought about the issue is that one old rule of thumb says to use articles with all nouns you can count. Many may find this sage advice to students whose first languages do not have articles. Thinking deeper about it, however, one realizes that the English article system is not simple at all for reasons discussed here in this chapter.

THE WHAT AND WHY OF ARTICLES

Before delving into the intricacies of the English article system, there are two questions to address: What are they? And why do they exist in the first place? The "what" of articles may be the simpler question. Grammarians call them **determiners**, and this designation is quite accurate. But what do they designate or determine? The most elegant answer, one discussed in depth below, is that articles "determine" a noun's specificity and importance.

The "why" of articles is a bit more complicated and quite fascinating, and has everything to do with cultural attitudes in general and Negotiated Perspective specifically. Think of it this way. Suppose that one lives in a culture that is fairly homogeneous, one where community identity is strong, and where individuals within that community are — as an assemblage — committed to preserving community values and behaviors. Now, suppose these community values and the ways of behaving have been passed down from generation to generation to the extent that the sense of community and appropriate behavior is well-ingrained and automatic. In that culture, whenever people have a conversation, since they share the same values and ways of behaving, they do not need to say everything because most things cultural are assumed. They let the other person in the conversation infer what is being said behind the words, what is important and what is not. In that culture, they do not need to be overly specific because the context of the conversation itself as well as their shared cultural values determine what is specific and not, what is important and not.

Now, by contrast, suppose that one lives in a culture that is very diverse, a culture where there are communities comprised of individuals from a variety of cultural backgrounds, each with unique values and behaviors. Moreover, that culture gives greater weight to the sanctity of the individual. Individuals are encouraged to "think for themselves" and establish their own uniqueness within the confines of the general values and behaviors of the culture at large. Since this culture is highly individualistic, the conversations would naturally reflect the nature of the community.

Two people in a conversation together cannot automatically assume that the other can infer what is important in the discourse and what is not, apart from what is said, since their sense of shared community may not be the same. They have no basis on which to make assumptions, neither do they have sufficient context to make inferences about what is important and not important in the discourse. Therefore, they must provide the appropriate context to enable each other to understand what is on their minds. If a particular notion is specific, they have to tell the listener it is specific. If a particular notion is important, they have to indicate to the other that it is important. If a notion is not specific nor important, they have to let the other in on that, too.

Intercultural specialists William Gudykunst and Young Kim give the two types of cultures we discussed above names. The first example they term **high context cultures**, and the second example, **low context cultures**. They define the difference this way: "High context communication can be characterized as being indirect, ambiguous, and understated, with speakers being reserved and sensitive to listeners. Low context communication, in contrast, can be characterized as being direct, explicit, open, precise, and consistent with one's feelings."[1]

It is little accident that languages which are spoken by persons from high context cultures, usually those with an orientation toward collectivism, as Gudykunst and Kim designate them, do not have articles — for example, such cultures and languages as Japanese, Chinese, Swahili, Arabic, etc. The one real exception is the Spanish and Portuguese (low context languages) spoken in Latin America (comprised of generally high context cultures). But one could just as easily argue that the languages spoken in Latin America were imported from European cultures with a more low context orientation, and the high context cultures have adapted the language to their culture. Most native Amerindian languages in North and South America — Quechua, Aymara, Nahuatl, and Cherokee being examples — have no explicit article system.

It is not that speakers in high context cultures have no way of being explicit. For example, Swahili has words meaning "this person or thing" and "that person or thing" when speakers need to point out this or that. Rather, explicitness in language is often not a high priority in high context cultures because persons engaged in conversations know if what is being discussed is specific or not. High context cultures are so structured that speakers only need provide the amount of information necessary to convey the message. It is up to the hearer to infer what is important and not important in a discourse. In fact, Gudykunst and Kim indicate that saying too much in a high context culture may be perceived as being "untrustworthy."

Articles in these languages only serve to get in the way. They are unnecessary grammatical vocabulary because the context of the conversation as well as the conversants' understanding of the culture at large and their inferences regarding what is important in the discourse and what is background information reveal what is explicit and what is not. By contrast, communication in low context cultures tends to be explicit. Clarity and precision are keys to understanding messages. What is important and what is not must be marked in language because there is not a strong sense of the "collective" (shared culture). Now, the point of this discussion is not to argue that there are no low context communities with low context conversations in high context cultures and vice versa. This is not an attempt to overgeneralize here. But suffice it to say that cultures display certain societal patterns of belief and behavior which designate them high or low context. The English language, being generally considered a low context language stemming from generally low context cultures, must explicitly indicate what is specific and important. English has the article system (those supposedly "simple" words *a, an* and *the*) to do this.

The Case Against Definite and Indefinite

Traditional grammarians, those who lean toward prescriptivism, will say with some confidence that there are two types of articles, a **definite article** and an **indefinite** one. The first is represented by *the*, and the latter by *a* if it precedes a consonantal sound or *an* if it precedes a vowel sound; simple enough. Grammarians further go to say that if something is real or tangible — which means if one can see it, touch it, smell it, taste it, hear it, etc., or if it is in the one-of-a-kind category — then chances are great it will take a definite article. The rest take indefinite articles or, in the case of generic nouns, no articles at all.

On the surface, this sounds like a reasonable rule of thumb. Certainly, it has been around for ages and ages and, in some English camps, is still the common mantra for explaining the English article system. Or it could be said that it *was* reasonable until University of Oregon linguist, Tom Givon, threw a proverbial monkey wrench into the "article" works. In his seminal work, *English Syntax*, Givon uses the following example to point out the problem (though the name has been changed):

> Julie wanted to marry a French sailor,
> but she didn't know him well.
> vs.
> Julie wanted to marry a French sailor,
> but she didn't know any.[2]

Givon goes on to explain that the *a* article in the first sentence is definitely definite while the *a* article in the second sentence is definitely indefinite. But notice here that the article does not change, only the degree of definiteness. How can there be a definite indefinite article, unless, of course, definiteness has little to do with the meaning of articles? Givon's pithy example not only demonstrates the difficulty of jumping to conclusions when it comes to articles, but illustrates the importance of discourse and context in enabling their understanding. It also points up the need for a new definition of what an article is and why they are used. By elucidating Givon's example, it will demonstrate how native English speakers "think" about articles.

The First Scenario

"Julie wanted to marry a French sailor, but she didn't know him well."

Picture it this way. Here's Julie, a Francophile from, say, Nebraska, who has been awarded a prestigious scholarship to study French linguistics for the summer at the University of Marseille. She travels to France, sees the sights of Paris, samples the finest wines and cheeses in Burgundy, does the beach scene on the Côte d'Azur, and finally settles into the routine of a student at the University of Marseille. One evening, while out with friends at a trendy Marseille nightclub, she meets Jean Yves Gourmand, a lieutenant in the French navy. They sweep each other off their collective feet, start spending their free time together, then fall in love to the extent that they begin talking about marriage. One evening, Jean Yves invites Julie to an expensive restaurant in Marseille. And over an expensive bottle of Moët & Chandon, Yves proposes marriage to Julie, a proposal she readily accepts. It is mid-July when the proposal is offered and accepted, but by mid-August, Julie begins questioning her decision to marry Jean Yves. She is concerned that she really doesn't know him well enough to marry him. By the time she is to leave, she is in such turmoil that she calls off the engagement and returns to Nebraska relieved but saddened.

The Second Scenario

"Julie wanted to marry a French sailor, but she didn't know any."

This one is a bit different. There is Julie, the Francophile from Nebraska, who was awarded a prestigious scholarship to study at the University of Marseille. As in the scenario above, she travels to France, sees the sights of Paris, samples the finest wines and cheeses in Burgundy, does the beach scene on the Cote d'Azure, and finally settles into the routine of a student at the University of Marseille. Marseille, being a port city, is home to French naval installations. Julie encounters many French sailors on her daily visits around the city, and she is quite struck by their looks and demeanor. In fact, Julie is so intrigued that she dreams of marrying one of these sailors, especially an officer. So she regularly parks herself at a small café on the waterfront, enjoys a coffee or two and watches the sailors pass. Unfortunately for Julie, her time in Marseille is mostly occupied with research and other tasks related to school, and the French sailors who pass by do not seem interested in the shy student from Marseille who regularly parks herself at the same table at the same time every day. So no matter how badly she wants to get to know a French naval officer, she has never been in the right place at the right time to actually meet one interested in meeting her. Her year in France passes without meeting a single French sailor, although she is still intrigued by them and fancies marrying one.

The Pyramid and the Möbius Strip

Given these two scenarios about Julie's adventures in France or lack thereof, how does one make sense of articles? Here is an example drawn from one of my classes those answers this. Three of my former students, Robb Jolly, Janice Wooten and Mary Farthing (who to this day collectively continue to be both perceptive and wise), postulated that the article system is really about the two related pragmatic notions, that of importance and specificity. Definiteness relates to both but does not encompass both. The idea is that the more specific something is the more important it likely is and vice versa, the less specific something is the less important it will be. The three developed a useful visual rubric to represent their theory.

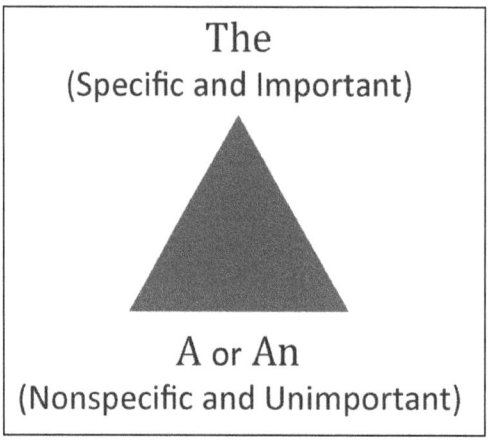

Figure 2: Article Pyramid: Scale of Specificity and Importance.[3] This figure shows the relationship between specificity and importance; the more specific something is, the more important it will be. This illustration was proposed by Rob Jolly, Janice Wooten, and Mary Farthing.

In this model, the bottom of the pyramid represents things and concepts which are not specific at all, and, consequently, not at all important. As one ascends the pyramid toward things and concepts which are more specific and important, the more likely one will shift article usage from *a* or *an* to *the*. What is important to remember here is that there is no set definition of what is specific and what is important. Nor is there any set black-and-white boundary where one will begin to use *the* versus *a* or *an*. The definition of importance and specificity is left up to the participants in the conversation as they negotiate meaning with one another. This even applies to one-of-a-kind realities like the moon or the World Series. Participants would very likely mutually agree that there is only one moon that revolves around the Earth, or that there is only one World Series played every year after the regular baseball season (at least in the United States). A conversation about Jupiter's moons would likely be different because Jupiter has more than one moon.

While the illustration of a pyramid is a helpful insight into the nature of the Negotiated Perspective of articles, the grammatical complexity of the nominal system of English necessitates an adaptation of the Jolly, Wooten and Farthing model. Moreover, while the illustration of a pyramid captures the scalar dimensions of the English article system, the diamond configuration (albeit an asymmetrical diamond) in the illustration below extends the pyramid in a second direction. Each endpoint of the diamond represents a null set, nouns which do not have articles. At the bottom of the diamond are generic nouns which are so non-specific and carry such a low level of importance that they do not take articles. At the top of the diamond are referential pronouns which bear the highest level of importance. These pronouns are so specific and important that they also do not need article determinants to further define them. The level of specificity and importance becomes greater toward the top of the diamond, and, vice versa, the level of specificity and importance becomes less toward the bottom of the diamond. As one moves up the diamond from generic, and as the level of specificity and importance increases, the more likely one will use an article

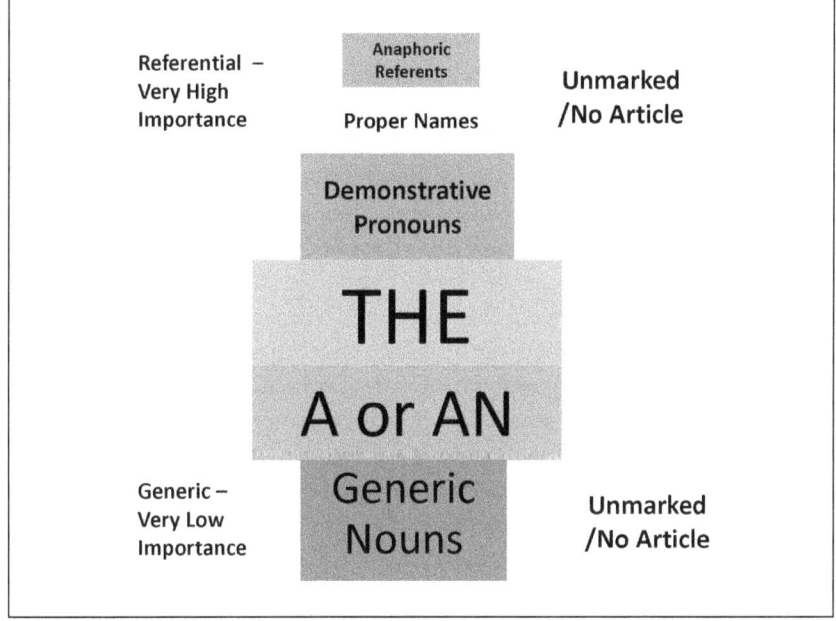

Figure 3: The Diamond. The diamond figure is an adaptation of Jolly, Wooten and Farthing. In this illustration, what is generic, non-specific, and likely unimportant (at the bottom of the diamond), do not take articles. At the top of the diamond are things, concepts, etc., that are so specific and important that they need no article because they are directly identified with a person or oneself.

until the point at which one will specify a noun with a demonstrative pronoun. Moving beyond demonstratives are proper names and anaphoric references (pronouns), neither of which are commonly marked with articles. The diamond is wider at the bottom to represent the larger class of nouns which carry low specificity and importance.

Another analogy which may help explain how articles function in common-usage communication (and literacy grammar, for that matter) is taken from the world of visual media. As was discussed in Chapter 1, **Perspective** can be metaphorically viewed as representing a movie or, more precisely, multiple movies, in a person's brain, a collective (although not processed collectively) of many memories and their associated emotions.

Suppose we are having a conversation about some event, say Julie's wanting to marry that French sailor. I have some idea about Julie, as do you. We probably share experiences with Julie. We may both know, for example, that Julie loves France, that she was afforded the opportunity to travel to France for the summer. We may both know that Julie was studying French or, specifically, that she was studying French in Marseille with a famous French linguist. But I have a piece of the "Julie" story that you do not have. I know that when Julie was in Marseille in mid-July, she met Jean Yves, a lieutenant in the French Navy, fell madly in love with him and wanted very much to marry him. I know that Jean Yves also fell in love with Julie and had popped the question, had given her a ring, and together, they had set a future wedding date. I also know that when Julie was about to leave France, she got cold feet and decided not to marry Jean Yves because she didn't know him well. I know this and you do not. I know this because I saw Julie the other day and she related the whole story to me. Julie's story, of course, has been interpreted through my own experience, through various experiences like those of being married, and the process one has to go through to get that way, memories of living in France during high school, experiences of sailors I have known personally or through the media, although I have never been a sailor myself in the United States or French Navy, and finally, my memories-cum-experiences of Julie, etc.

I want you to have a similar "picture" in your mind that I have in mine. But, as I am having this conversation with you, I must make several assumptions about what you know and do not know. These assumptions are critical for the success or failure of the conversation. I assume you have not heard the "French sailor" story, i.e., that piece is missing from your knowledge of Julie's France experience. The French sailor is real, a sentient and dedicated being named Jean Yves, therefore definite. In fact, there is no doubt about his definiteness either in my mind or in yours. What is in question here is the definiteness of your knowledge, or at least my assumption of the breadth of your knowledge. And so when I utter, "Julie wanted to marry a French sailor, but she didn't know him well," I am in a great sense negotiating meaning with you, or at least I am negotiating my assumptions with you. You could easily respond, "Yeah, I knew that. Julie told me yesterday." In this case, I would have to change my assumptions about you. "Oh, so you talked to Julie already? Wasn't that some experience she had!"

Figure 3 tries, in some sense, to illustrate how perspective is negotiated within the narrow viewpoint of article usage. Perhaps the image of a Möbius Strip may be a more appropriate representation. As it has no beginning and no end, speakers of English will use articles (or no articles at all) at different times depending upon the context in which they find themselves, and depending upon what they know or think they know about the other interlocutor. It is constantly changing. Starting in the middle of the Möbius Strip, where the lines overlap, one segment of the line represents objects and concepts which have some intimate identification with the speaker, called here "Self-Reference." Because of their intimate relationship with the speaker, these objects or concepts, represented usually as anaphoric (reference) pronouns like I, me, mine, need no article to determine their specificity and importance. The opposite segment of the same line (remember, a Möbius Strip is a continuous, unending line) are objects and concepts which have no exclusivity to the speaker whatsoever. They are generic, not identifiable to any particular individual. Therefore, no article is required because generic entities and ideas are neither specific nor important. However, when objects and concepts take on degrees of specificity and importance, articles are required in order that hearers or readers understand the degree of specificity and importance which the speaker wishes to convey. This is illustrated in the "outer perimeter" segments of the Möbius Strip.

A specific, and hopefully important, illustration is in order here. You are thirsty, and decide to stop by McLaren's Tavern after work. You know from experience that McLaren's is famous for their many varieties of beer. At this moment, you do not have any specific beer in mind, but it being a hot summer day, and since you have just put in a nine-hour day at your job as a woodworker making an art-deco rocking chair, any beer will do just as long as it's cold. You have also made arrangements to meet your buddy Karl after work. Karl arrives before you, and is equally hot and thirsty. So he orders himself two ice-cold Roseman Wheat Lagers, the first of which he is enjoying when you arrive. You see Karl at a table across the room, and you notice he has two beers (see below, The Problem with Count and Mass). "Great," you say to yourself, "Karl has already gotten me a beer." (At this point you do not know which kind of beer it is; it's one of McLaren's 250 varieties, but you and Karl have been friends for a long time, so that number is narrowed to ten at most.) You go over, shake hands and sit, and by this time, your mouth is watering to dive into the glass of beer Karl has ordered for you ("the" is used with "glass" because it is specific and important to the occasion, since it is the one you are about to drink). So, without hesitation, you point and say "Mine?" Karl replies, "Yep, yours!" No article needed. The beer in question belongs to you, it is identified as yours. Karl goes on to say, "It's a new Roseman Lambic, blackberry." ("A" is required here because you do not know yet what is in your glass; only Karl and Danny, the barkeep, know. So to you, your quaff is a non-specified type.) You reply, "This lambic is great!" "This," one of English's demonstrative pronouns, is of very high specificity and importance, more so than "the."

Therefore, to summarize the significance of articles, these seemingly insignificant words are quite significant in that they say a lot about what people assume about themselves and the people with whom they are having a conversation. They are also significant for another reason. They define, in some sense, the world people live in, and more specifically, the culture people claim as their own. Articles give people a sense of what is assumed to be real, tangible and significant in the world. Definitely!

Next, there will be discussion about three interesting and puzzling uses of articles: first, counting mass nouns; second, the use of *the* with certain nations; and third, a peculiar case where the article *a* is used with the non-specific noun *man* and can mean something both specific and non-specific at the same time, of course depending upon the culture a person is in.

The Problem with Count and Mass

You go into a bar after a long day's work and sidle up to the counter. The bartender comes over to you and says, "What'll you have?" And the first words out of your mouth send you into grammatical purgatory: "Gimme a beer." Suppose the bartender is also a traditional grammarian moonlighting to get some extra cash (grammarians have never been known to be among the high wage earners). "Whadda ya mean, 'Gimme a beer?' You can't count beer. Beer is a mass noun. So much for *your* grammatical training, Bub." So after you down a few and leave shamed, without leaving a tip, you wander aimlessly down the street. Suddenly, as if struck by something you've always known, you say to yourself, "I sure as heck can say, 'Gimme a beer!'" And indeed, you sure as heck can. And so you go back and offer a non-prescriptive answer to the barkeep, who proceeds to have you thrown out by a 300-pound weightlifter with no neck.

The problem here has been correctly described as one of semantic intention, meaning more than you are saying. Another way of stating the problem, in terms of the **Mascagni Effect**, would be, how does the brain understand quantities? When ordering that beer, you no doubt meant that you wanted beer served in a bottle or in a frosted mug, or if you frequent certain more informal places, a plain old can. You did not intend for the bartender to come over and pour a quantity of beer (which *is* countable, incidentally) directly into your mouth or on the table so you could lap it up like a dog. Although you might find that sort of activity commonly happening during a college spring break ritual, you are not usually looking for that kind of service in the quotidian round of bar hopping. Nor would you expect that behavior.

So what is the issue here? Fortunately, there is nothing major involved here, just the simple matter of the human brain being able to understand and process the present context to the extent that one is able to "count" traditional mass nouns. And the simple fact that it really does not matter whether some hypothetical container exists in some hypothetical deep structure somewhere; what matters is that language is wonderfully economical and the human brain is marvelously efficient. Brains of English speakers and hearers can readily parse and negotiate the meaning of these expressions. So whether it is beer, milk, wine (as in, I would like two white wines to go with this fine scaloppini di vitello) or some other mass of substance, count away!

Islands (or Icelands) in the Stream

One of the most interesting facets of English nouns is what happens to countries and islands, especially countries which are, at the same time, islands. People can say, for example, *the* United States or *the* Philippines or *the* Seychelles, but we do not say *the* Japan, *the* Iceland, or *the* Australia when perfectly reasonable and interesting languages such as Portuguese can do just that. Why?

English actually does allow *the* Japan, Iceland, and Australia and so on in defined contexts. Suppose you were born and raised in Iceland, and as a child, you used to frolic in the hot springs, walk with your parents on the glaciers, enjoy the aurora borealis on cold winter nights. You left Iceland at age 15 and moved to the United States. Just last year, at age 30 you returned, and you found that outside the hot springs you used to frequent, some entrepreneur had put up a McDonald's, the glaciers had receded, and the light show to which you were accustomed had been blocked out by incessant lights from Reykjavik and Keflavik and two or three other Viks that have sprung up since you moved. One night, after a particularly crowded and unpleasant light-filled frolic in the hot springs, you returned to your hotel and commented to the English-speaking concierge who had arranged the frolic, "This isn't *the* Iceland I remember," a very specific time in a very specific place, changed forever.

But back to the question at hand. As was mentioned before, both language and the brain are very economical and efficient. There is often little need to express everything when the community of speakers generally assumes what you assume. For example, there is little reason to formulate most countries like Germany as being more specific when it is assumed to be a specific sociopolitical unit. In other words, "Germany" itself carries specificity. The problem arises when there are scattered islands which comprise a political unit, such as the myriad of large and small islands that make up the Philippines, or a number of relatively semi–self-governing states that comprise the union known as the United States. In these cases, "the" brings the disparate into a whole. That is, native speakers of American English understand that it is important that the United States is comprised of individual states, while at the same time, they are comfortable in acknowledging the fact that the United States has a centralized government. Likewise, for such multi-island nations as Palau and Indonesia, which do not take *the*, people inherently have come to understand in context that, while these nations have numerous sociopolitical entities, they think it important to view the nation as a unified whole. They're not concerned with how Sarawak is governed. Perhaps this is true because these nations themselves have established the importance of viewing themselves as a unity, whereas, as in the case of the United States, Americans have established it as important for others to view them in terms of *e pluribus unum*, "Out of many, one." Again, the notions of specificity and importance appear to be the salient factors in the naming of theses political entities, and whether or not they are viewed as collectives or multiples.

The Strange Case of "A Man"

As has been stressed and will continue to be stressed, issues of grammar have cultural significance. Cultural significance may indeed lie at the heart of most of not all grammatical "choice." The meaning of articles used in everyday speech is no exception. Take the following conversation.[4]

Two men are sitting behind the counter at a filling station in Boone, North Carolina, in the heart of the Appalachian Mountains. One is the attendant, and the other is his buddy who is in the National Guard and has stopped in briefly to visit. The National Guardsman is reading an article in the *Charlotte Observer* about two men who were canoeing on a rain-swollen creek in eastern North Carolina, missed their pick-up point and had to be rescued by helicopter. It seems that the canoeists were having such a good time that they decided to paddle a few more miles down the river. And that's where they ran into real serious, life-threatening trouble. We pick up the conversation:

> GUARDSMAN: "And these two guys *missed* the people who 'us supposed to pick 'em up. The people were standing right there yellin' at 'em, and they paddled right by! And then they had to be rescued by the National Guard." (laughing).
>
> ATTENDANT: "Well, you'd think a man wouldn't do anything dumb like that."

What is going on here in terms of the **Mascagni Effect**? What does the article in *a man* mean in this context? Is it specific or non-specific? To answer these questions with any certainty, one must look at the culture from whence the conversation took place.

In the Appalachian Mountain regions of the southern United States, and for that matter in most of the entire southern region of the United States, politeness is taught as one of the most important codes in human interaction. In North Carolina, many mothers and fathers tell their children on quite a regular basis that if they do not have something nice to say about somebody, they ought not say anything at all. This notion probably ought to be enshrined in every school and public building in the South because it is certainly enshrined in the minds of every Southerner even if he or she does not always practice it. The "say-something-nice" canon is often paired with another value which says, "It is not polite to talk about someone behind their back." This one, too, is often ignored, especially when there is a juicy bit of gossip that needs to get out.

So here you have two southern men in one part of North Carolina discussing two other southern men, whom they did not know, from another part of North Carolina. Now, according to the "rules" of southern etiquette, it is okay to talk about the canoers, even if is behind their backs, because it is a matter of public information; the information was, after all, in the newspaper. The guys at the filling station were not gossiping. Nor were they being terribly impolite. Continuing to canoe down a swiftly-flowing flooded river while drinking beer and partying would probably be considered rather "shortsighted" by anyone's definition. So, in this instance, the canoers were fair game! That's probably why the attendant called them "dumb," or at least called their actions "dumb."

But there is something else going on here, the not-so-small matter of making a public pronouncement about the way the world operates or should operate according to the values of the community from whence the pronouncement issues forth. "You'd think a man wouldn't do anything dumb like that." The pronouncer was indeed specifically referring to the particular men in the canoe that day. Those particular men should not have gone off and done that particular deed and gotten themselves into a particular situation where good taxpayer money was used to pluck them out of a tree. The pronouncer was also referring to something non-specific at the same time, the general rule of thumb which guides appropriate behavior maintaining safe communities. The rule of thumb would be something like this: "In general, it is wise not to drink excessively, and is not wise not to canoe rain-swollen creeks at flood stage. And if you do those things, it is wise to tell someone, perhaps including the authorities in charge of safety for the region, you are doing it and have an appropriate responsible person waiting at the other end to pick you up, or in the case of the likely emergency, rescue you." That's what "You'd think a man wouldn't do anything dumb like that" means. In this case, the *a* in *a man* is both specific and non-specific, and in both cases, it is important to be said and for all in earshot to hear.

Now You Try It!

1. Islands in the Stream Revisited

As was discussed above, in English, certain multi-island or multi-state nations contain the article "the" in their names (for example, "the United States," "the Philippines" and "the Seychelles"), while country names, for the most part, do not have an article before the name (for example, France, Japan and Brazil). Consider why this is so. Come up with an explanation based on Negotiated Perspective that explains both country names possessing an article and country names that do not.

2. Telling Stories

Articles have to do with the assumptions speakers and hearers make about the specificity and importance of something, be it a thing, concept or event. Recall something that happened to you recently. Tell someone who was not privy to the event the story, but tell it assuming the other person has knowledge of the event. What happens as the discourse is shared? Now tell the story to someone who *was* privy to the event. Only this time, tell it as if the person has *no* knowledge of the event. What happens as this second discourse is shared?

3
Prepositions: It's Above Smitty's!

THE QUESTION

The difficulty of prepositions was brought home to me by four events. These four seemingly innocuous events convinced me that of all the grammatical aspects of English, prepositions may be among the most difficult for non-native speakers to grasp (and perhaps for native speakers as well), but may be the quintessential example of how **Negotiated Perspective** operates in human communication.

The first event happened to me when I was nine or 10 years old. At that age, I dreamed of becoming an airplane pilot. That dream was so strong that I became absolutely obsessed by aviation, and I still am to some extent. The greatest joy in my young life was a trip to the airport to watch the planes take off and land, and occasionally go on board before the passengers boarded (it helped that my father worked for Capital Airlines, later merged with United), so being able to go on board an airplane was not only possible, but it often happened (this was long before the strict security measures that all but makes this utterly impossible). Since I could not physically fly — I was not born with wings nor was I of the age to take flying lessons — I was able to live out my aviation fantasy by building model airplanes.

It just so happened that one of the first gigantic pre–Walmart mega-discount stores, called Met, opened to great fanfare near my neighborhood. My mother scoped the Met out, and returned with the report that the model section was rife with many types of airliners. I could hardly wait to go. Wanting more information, I asked my mother where the Met was. She replied without hesitation, "It's above Smitty's (our local filling station, curiously named for the mechanic who worked there and not the owner) and the Main Street Drive-in (the local theater)." Now when my mother said that the Met was above Smitty's, my little mind envisioned the store being up in the air over the station, and we had the following conversation, remembered as best I can.

"Where do you park?" I asked my mother.

She got a curious look on her face and said, "Why, in the parking lot. Where else?"

"Well, how do you get into the store?"

The curious look turned even more curious, as if I had fallen from my bike and hit my head, and knocked myself cuckoo. "You go right in the door. Why do you ask?"

"You said it was above Smitty's. How can a store be up in the air?" I queried.

"Oh, silly, the store is not up in the air. It is just past Smitty's on the right, a little beyond the Main Street Drive-in."

"Oh, so it's not up in the air?" I just wanted a bit more clarification and affirmation.

"No, it's not in the air. I guess I'll have to show you."

And so we went to the Met, which was, as she said, just a little past ("above") Smitty's and the Main Street Drive-in. I came away from that trip with a nice TWA Constellation which I built secure in the knowledge that airliners fly and stores do not.

Decades later, one of my star students, a young woman named Patricia who happened also to be a "crackerjack" CPA from Mexico, was supposed to pick up her roommate, who took the local bus to Walmart one evening to pick up a few items. The arrangement was that her roommate would call for Patricia to come pick her up when she was finished shopping. So the roommate called...

"I'm finished with my shopping. Can you come and pick me up?"

"Where are you?"

"I'm at Walmart," was the answer.

Patricia asked, "Well, where at Walmart?"

"Excuse me?"

"Where at Walmart?"

"I'm in Walmart right now, cameras I think. Just meet me at Walmart."

"But where?"

"In the front, where else?"

The story ends happily with the student being collected near the front door of Walmart. The next day, the topic of conversation in class was prepositions. "**What is the difference between being at Walmart and in Wal-**

mart? Aren't they the same?" I was struck by the question. Of course they are not the same. The two are not even the same for Patricia, that is, she knows the difference between being enclosed by the Walmart (being in the store) and being outside the Walmart, standing in front waiting to be picked up. At its core, her question can be rephrased this way: "Why use two different prepositions when one will do?" In effect, "I know I cannot drive my car into the Walmart. I just want to know where to pick you up." For the roommate, Patricia's question perhaps struck her as being a strange one. "Why do you need to know where I am at Walmart at this very moment? All you need to know is that I am ready to be picked up."

The third event occurred soon thereafter, after we as a class had discussed prepositions in light of the Walmart incident, and after I assumed we had prepositions down pretty well. One of my students from China chimed into a conversation on directions by asking about prepositions and modes of transportation. Her question struck at the heart of the problem with prepositions in English: there are many of them and their meanings often overlap. How is it that can you be *on* the plane and *in* the plane at the same time? How can you be *on* the bus when you are *in* the bus? I will discuss this persistent problem a bit later.

The final event occurred when a colleague of mine from Japan stopped me in the hall with the following query: "Where does *in spite of* come from? We have nothing like that in Japanese. Besides, what does spite mean? And how can you be inside of it?" My colleague's query raises the almost undecipherable problem of the idiomatic uses of prepositional phrases and phrasal verbs. This subject will also be discussed in this chapter.

But before one can be enlightened regarding how Negotiated Perspective works with prepositions, one should first take a general look at the strange behavior of these small, seemingly inconsequential modifiers.

Strange Behavior

While there are a myriad of grammatical snares in the English language waiting to pounce upon some unsuspecting student, none of the snares offers more headaches than prepositions. Semester by semester by semester, students ask that this great mystery be unlocked, as if somehow prepositions *en masse* had been deposited in a beautiful bejeweled trunk, only the key to the lock has been lost. In their eyes, opening this trunk would reveal marvels too wonderful for the eyes to behold, and one of those marvels would be the key to understanding English. What is interesting is that opening this particular trunk *is* one of the keys to understanding English for reasons that will be explained in a moment.

It is not as if students do not know how to use prepositions. That is to say, it is not that students do not know where they go in a sentence. They get that part right almost all the time. The problem is which one to use when. For the Mexican CPA in the story above, it matters little whether she is *in* Walmart or *at* Walmart; she uses the same preposition in Spanish, *en*. What if she is *on* a ship? *En*. What if she is *in* a taxi? *En*. What if she is riding *on* a bus? *En*. How about if she is mounted on top of one of those uncomfortable narrow bicycle seats, pedaling with all her might like Lance Armstrong trying to win the Vuelta de España? *En*.

The same goes for Japanese as well. Whether you are in or at Walmart, you would say the same thing, *Waru-Marto ni* (the postposition in this case indicating specific location or goal of motion) *imasu* (the verb "to be"). How is a student supposed to know which one to use when English has at least 20 prepositions to choose from, and his or her native language only has three or four? And to add insult to injury, how can the selection be made efficiently and effectively when these multiple prepositions have multiple meanings?

To illustrate this, pick any preposition. Pick — for the sake of argument — *in*, which is one of the English equivalents of the Spanish preposition *en*, or the Japanese postposition *ni*. *In* can mean literally "inside of," spatially bounded by walls, as in, "Your coat is where you left it last time you wore it! *In* the closet. Did you look for it?"

Coupled with this notion of spatial boundedness, *in* can also denote being situationally bound, as if inside of some emotional, psychic, or otherwise expressional state of being. "In anger," "in heat," "in pain" and "in cahoots with" are good examples of this. He answered the question about his questionable coaching strategy *in* anger. An animal *in* heat is looking to mate because the time to mate has arrived. Anyone who has ever been *in* pain knows how encompassing and absorbing the misery of pain can often be. Someone *in* cahoots with someone else is emotionally, physically and — sometimes — criminally entwined with that other person, usually with no redeeming intention.[1]

Likewise, *in* can denote a period of time, specific and/or non-specific. "When does class begin?" "*In* ten minutes" (a specific period of time). "When will you take me to get that new bike?" "*In* a few minutes" (a non-specific period of time). As an aside, where I grew up, which is down South, it is impolite to tell someone "no way" outright, or in the case above, "Quit bothering me, there is no way I will take you to get any bike, new or old."

So, for generations, we have used indirect ways of saying "no," such as "*in* a few minutes" or "*after* while" (another good preposition to ponder) which may be now or 20 years from now, or "we'll see" which means no way in hell. Some other interesting examples of *in* used to tell time are: *in* the nick of time (whatever a nick is), *in* a flash (real quick) and *in* a heartbeat (real quick).

Direction is the third common function of *in*. "*In* exchange" may be the best example. "*In* exchange for her valuable information, the police offered her a nice reward." There is a sense of direction here, mutual direction, something given for something received. Another example is "*in* reverse." "How do you expect to get out of this parking lot if you don't put this thing [the car] *in* reverse?"

Then there are the *in* anomalies. "As *in*" is one, meaning "meaning." "Take the phrase 'fur piece,' as *in*, 'she lives a "fur piece" down the road' ('far' for the non–Southerners)." Another is "*in* tow," meaning "to bring along not necessarily by choice." "I've got my husband '*in* tow' for this flower show. He swore he would never go to another one, but he relented after I told him he could buy that new truck." Another is "*in* a pickle," meaning "trouble" or difficulty. "I haven't finished my project, and now I am *in* a pickle." "*In* response" is another, meaning "I will answer your question. I may not want to answer it, but I will." "*In* response to your question, I feel that we should not dump that much money into education" (incidentally, this is a direct quote from a politician from one of the least educated states in the United States — the state's name will go unmentioned). And there is "*in* conclusion," meaning "the end"!

And *in* is just one example. There are 20-odd more prepositions, each with multiple meanings. Some of these many meanings can be easily categorized using time, space, direction, and manner distinctions. But for every clear-cut definition, for every denotation that can be categorized, there are at least 10 others that defy categorization. How then can one make sense of prepositions?

THE ZEN OF PREPOSITIONS

Combining two paradigms may be able to clear up many of the difficulties presented by prepositions, although, admittedly, no one solution may be sufficient to explain every instance of prepositional use. The first is one of this handbook's main themes, the **Mascagni Effect**, and the second, which is an important related theme, **Narrative Imaging**.

Space, Time, Direction and the Mascagni Effect

Negotiated Perspective may be the key to understanding how prepositions work in everyday discourse. Prepositions, at least those which are not idiomatic, are first and foremost markers of one person's perspective in time and space and sometimes direction, in relation to the perspective of another person in relation to the location of an object or idea in real time and space. Sound confusing? Well, it is! But take heart; prepositions in most languages work this way.

Look at it another way. Suppose you want me to get an item for you, say the latest thriller by the Spanish writer Arturo Perez-Reverte. You know that the book is on the bookshelf near the door next to the Thomas Harris book. Now picture the fact that there are bookshelves on both sides of the door, both about two feet from the door. When you say, "Rick, go get me the Perez-Reverte book on the shelf next to the door," you assume I know which shelf you are talking about. Now suppose I am situated in the room so that one bookshelf (doesn't matter which) appears closer to the door than the other. Since you said that the book is on the shelf "next to" the door, I assume that you mean the one that is closer to the door from *my* perspective, so I go scrounging around the bookshelf, searching in vain for *The Flanders Panel*. "No! No! No! Not that bookshelf [the one I am browsing through]! *That* bookshelf!" And you point to a bookshelf on the other side of the door. And then I realize that, in fact, you mean the one closer to the door from *your* perspective, which may or may not be the same bookshelf that is nearer to me, depending on where you are located in the room.

Try to appreciate the difficulty perspective naturally brings to discourse. Not only do prepositions have to do with perspectives, but also with assumptions about the perspective of the person with whom one is speaking. As discovered previously, communication is, in part, motivated by the assumptions made of the perspective of the person with whom one is conversing. Those assumptions may be accurate, in which case the other person will affirm the accuracy of the assumption. At other times, assumptions are not accurate, at which time the interlocutor will correct them.

Suppose I am standing in my seminar classroom a bit behind (approximately three feet) and to the right side of the desk in the room. In this classroom, there are six chairs, each occupied by one of my students. I ask the class, "Am I standing next to the desk?" Alex, seated a bit to my right, indicates that I am nearer the desk than I am to the student on his left, my immediate right, but that I am not "next to" the desk.

Tamara, seated to my left, across the room from Alex, disagrees. She points out that I am actually behind the desk *and* next to the desk. To which Alex responds that I am not anywhere "next to the desk," at which point Tamara leaves her seat, goes over to where Alex is seated, and confirms that I am, indeed not "next to" the desk. Alex, in turn, moves to Tamara's seat, which confirms that, indeed, I am both behind and next to the desk.

To further illustrate this, I play a little game with my non-native English speakers each semester when they bring up the difficulty with prepositions, especially in relation to size and location. In this case, I commonly ask the students to sit at tables, and ask them to have a normal conversation. I circulate among them, taking photos from various perspectives. Figures 4 through 8 illustrate this exercise. The photos are of students in my English classes at the Université of Angers, France. In this example (Figure 4), a group of friends from the Université of Angers are in the campus cafeteria having a conversation between classes. Where is Liza? Photos illustrating the conversation are shown from a variety of angles.

"Where's Liza?" (Figure 4)

A variety of answers are possible. Liza is next to Yong Jie; Yong Jie is behind Liza; across from Roxane; to the right of Yong Jie.

"Where is Liza?" (Figure 5)

In this example, the perspective shifts ninety degrees. The camera angle is behind Liza, which places Yong Jie in closer proximity. We discover, in this perspective, that Yong Jie is not seated at all, but standing next to Liza. Roxane, across from Liza, appears to Liza's left. Ludivine Le Maléfant, the fourth student at the table, is seated in front of and slightly to the right of Liza.

"Where is Liza now?" (Figure 6)

In this perspective, we are looking at Liza's conversation from an adjacent table. Liza is now to the right of Ludivine, even though she is seated to her left.

In this exercise, it is common to have a wide disparity of opinions, and disagreements as to the exact location of an object in a defined space at a defined time, especially since perspectives are continually in motion, shifting in time and space. What is interesting here is that the students' perspectives keep changing. This experiment points out the non-binary nature of prepositional perspective, that the definition of location, direction, and time depends upon the negotiated perspectives of the interlocutors.

3. Prepositions

Figure 4: Prepositions in Motion — Where's Liza? Liza Le-Bohec is seated in the campus lunchroom having a conversation with her friends. In this photograph, Liza is at left, wearing a striped shirt, Li Yong Jie is seated with her. Out of the picture are Roxane Lignel, across the table from Liza, and Ludivine Le Maléfant, seated near the paper on the table.

Figure 5: Prepositions in Motion — Point of View 1. Liza (in dark pants and light striped shirt) is seated next to Yong Jie (drinking from cup), Roxane (in glasses) is across from Liza and Ludivine (seated) is partially visible at the right.

3. Prepositions

Figure 6: Prepositions in Motion — Point of View 2. Liza's conversation from a neighboring table. Liza is seated to the left of Ludivine (in white shirt); to the right of Yong Jie (in jean jacket); and diagonally from Alyssa Mette (foreground), who is seated at a different table.

Stories, Schema, Prepositions and Phrasal Verbs

So far so good. Prepositions are about constantly shifting perspective. Using the metaphor of **Negotiated Perspective**, a preposition's spatial, temporal and directional connotation can be readily understood. However, two issues remain. First, how does one decide which preposition to use, and, second, how does one make sense of prepositions used metaphorically or idiomatically, which present a far wider range of problems? What can one make of such prepositional phrases as *on time, in spite of,* or the many phrasal verbs one encounters on a daily basis such as *turn on, chill out, come across, run into, get over, run around on* or other idiomatic phrases such as *like death warmed over*? Can one even go so far as to make any generalizations about these grammatical forms?

Before launching into a discussion of metaphor, schema and other neuro-cognitive issues, here is a word about phrasal verbs. First, phrasal verbs make up a large percentage of conversational verbs. Speakers of English use them all the time, mostly in informal conversation. Second, phrasal verbs consist of a verb that has one range of meaning and a preposition that has, no doubt, multiple meanings. What interesting is that when the verb and preposition are combined, the resulting verb phrase means something different from the verb and the preposition alone.

While it is almost impossible to generalize every single idiomatic use of English prepositions, the notion of **Narrative Imaging** may be a useful paradigm to understand how native English speakers "think prepositionally," in other words, how the brain configures prepositions in communication. This approach has its roots in an interesting study by linguist Mark Turner, elucidated in his book, *The Literary Mind*. Professor Turner explains that human beings make sense of the world through what he terms "basic stories." Basic stories are experiences of events in time and space. "The wind blows clouds through the sky, a child throws a rock, a mother pours milk into a glass, a whale swims through the water. These stories constitute our world and they are completely absorbing...."[2] These stories (interpretation of events, one's perspective of experiences) are consigned to highly complex neural networks, which, in turn, are linked together with other complex neural networks. These stories are, in Turner's view, "unproblematic" and automatic in that humans are "wired" to construct these stories. "We are built to learn to distinguish objects and events and combine them in small spatial stories."[3]

What is more, these basic stories recur over and over in the brain, comprising **Image Schema**, which is defined by Turner as "the categorization of experience, with each experience being somewhat different (i.e., perspective)."[4] Turner explains this notion of "image schema" this way:

> If we think of how often we reach out to pick up a glass and under what different conditions the event takes place, we see how varied the actual event is in its exact details each time it occurs. Our bodies are at slightly different orientations to the glass; the glass is slightly nearer or farther away; the glass sits on a slightly different surface; there may be obstructions to be avoided; the glass has a slightly different shape or weight or texture. We recognize all of the individual events of picking up a glass as belonging to one category in part because they all share a skeletal complex image schema.[5]

From people's earliest experiences, they are neurally put together in such a way as to store each different perspective of an event, connect them together, and, most fascinating, project them onto other stories, some similar and some different, to create a new story, a process Turner calls **Parable**. This projection occurs recursively so that one can combine almost any story to create a new perspective.

For example, take the phrase *like death warmed over*. Everyone has a basic story where death is the theme. Perhaps one knows someone who has died. Perhaps one has attended a funeral. That image schema with all its inherent stories combines with the image schema of warming combined with the schema of actions which are repetitive, and the combined story is a new reality.

Think of this way. You go to raid the fridge late one night, and all you see is that box of cold pizza which has been in the fridge for nigh on a week or so when your cousin Vinnie came over and left you with a half-eaten pizza and the tab for dinner. Now you crave something to eat, and the fridge is bare, and Vinnie's pizza is the only food available. So you pop a slice or two in the microwave, and what comes out is akin to eating an Italian-seasoned sponge. It's hot, but tastes *warmed over*—stale like it has been through the microwave a time or two. So you have the concept of warmed over and the concept of death. So you combine the two, and get something akin to the grim reaper who is walking on both feet, but looks right sickly—*death warmed over*; someone who looks like he or she is about to give up the ghost (another great phrasal verb phrase meaning to die): pale, waxen, with circles under the eyes, but still able to sit up and take nourishment—like *death warmed over*. The process of linking image schemas comprised of a lifetime's worth of basic stories applies to any idiomatic prepositional phrase or phrasal verb.

Transportational Problems

How one can be both *in* and *on* a plane can be explained through **Narrative Imaging**. People have image schema dealing with movement, manipulation and control. People have image schema which delineate someone who acts on someone or something, and schema that delineate someone or something being acted upon. People have size schema. People have experience of the scalar notions of largeness and smallness. The coalescence of those image schema create neuro-cognitive scenarios wherein one can conceive of oneself physically aboard a large mode of transportation, say a 777, not being in control of the jetliner (thankfully leaving the flying to an experienced pilot), flying through the air at mach .8.

Figure 7: *On* the Plane *In* the Air. A US Airways flight just before takeoff at the Charlotte-Douglas International Airport on a beautiful early October afternoon. When this picture was snapped, the passengers were *on* the plane and, in a few seconds, *in* the air. Upon arrival to wherever the Airbus was bound, the jet will touch down gently rendering the passengers, still *on* the plane, safely *on* the ground!

On the plane encompasses those multiple schema, but your location relative to the plane is not very important. *In* the plane encompasses different schema, although some schema overlap. Here, you may still be aboard a

3. Prepositions

Figure 8: Size Matters? I. Boone, North Carolina, is served by Appalcart, shown here in this photograph. Because of its size, compared to other types of transportation such as a car, you are *on* the bus when you ride it. In some countries, commuters often literally ride *on* the bus, that is, on top of it. So no matter whether you have a seat inside or are forced to ride on top, holding on for dear life, you are still *on* the bus. The exception is an 18-wheeler. If you are driving cross-country with a load of, say, fine Italian sports cars, and someone calls and asks you where you are, you say "I'm in my rig right now." This anomaly may have to do with the fact that the cab, while connected to the rest of the truck, is small by comparison to the trailer.

South African Airways 747-400, winging your way toward Cape Verde, not being in control of the plane, flying through the air at mach .8. However, one additional schema comes into play as being the most important, that of physical location with respect to the airplane. You are inside of it, not on the wings nor the vertical stabilizer.

The same problem can occur with sitting, as illustrated on the following page. A sofa schematically represents a physically large chair (Figure 10). And like being seated aboard a jetliner (although on most jetliners not so comfortably), where there is less of a sense of being in a narrow enclosed space, sitting *on* a couch is perceived differently from sitting *in* a chair (Figure 10).

Figure 9: Seated Prepositions — On the Bench. Here (left to right) Liza Le-Bohec, Roxane Lignel, Li Yong Jie and Ludivine Le Maléfant enjoy the warmth of a spring morning *on* a bench in front of the Faculté des Langues, Litteratures et Science Humaines, Université of Angers.

Figure 10: Seated Prepositions — In the Chair. Ludivine (left) and Liza chat between classes. They are seated *in* chairs.

PREPOSITIONS, PHRASAL VERBS AND WORLD VIEW

To review, high context cultures employ an economy of language because there seems to be a mutual understanding of the shared values and behaviors among members of the community. It is not necessary for collective cultures to express every single aspect of an event or situation; it is not important to implicitly reveal every important topic of a conversation. Persons from high context cultures can inherently fill in the blanks. Low context cultures use the opposite strategy. Context, the important details surrounding an event, is coded in language somewhat like providing someone with an explicit, highly detailed road map.

Let me illustrate how this works, or does not work, with an event that happened to me some years ago and involved receiving a set of directions. The event was extraordinary because it involved the person giving the directions using hyper-low context discourse when a high context discourse was completely appropriate. A colleague of mine and I had a luncheon appointment off campus. He phoned to tell me he would pick me up. The conversation went something like this: "It's 11:45 right now. I am leaving my office. I will drive from the parking lot at Raley Hall up Rivers Street. And in six minutes, I will drive up Locust Street and go around the circle next to the Student Union. If you would go down to the second floor, there is a porte-cochere on the north side of the building. I will pick you up at the porte-cochere." Now, just for the record, I enter that same porte-cochere every working day of the year, so I am quite familiar with its location. Moreover, how he gets to the porte-cochere is not particularly relevant. What is relevant is that he will get there at an approximate time and that he will give me a ride to our appointment. It would have been just as easy to say, "Meet me outside the second floor in five minutes."

If one considers high and low context conversations, prepositional use or non-use makes sense. In high context languages, prepositional use is economical, and so there is a tendency for the forms to coalesce. This may explain why languages like Japanese, Chinese, and even Spanish have fewer prepositional or postpositional forms. The reverse is true of languages commonly spoken in low context cultures, languages like English and German. There tends to be more forms with multiple meaning so that speakers can fully elucidate the context of an event in language.

Summing Up

In this examination of prepositions, it has been discovered that prepositions encompass three important features: First, connected spatial stories (image schema) are learned experientially; second, human experience is filtered through the many aspects of culture; third, prepositions carry not only image schematic information but cultural information as well, which is likely why they are so difficult to learn. Perhaps the easiest way to learn prepositions is to get into the head of a native speaker. How hard can that be?

Now You Try It!

1. Definitions

List as many meanings of these prepositions as you can.

at	before	from	through
about	below	in	to
above	between	of	toward(s)
against	by	on	under
around	for	over	with

2. Teaching Prepositions

Given what you have learned about prepositions, your task is to (1) write a brief explanation/summary of the function of prepositions in English, and (2) design two activities to illustrate the explanation. Nota bene — your explanation must be able to be grasped by a group of ESL students.

> **Context:** The English for International Students class at Pembrotanck University. The class consists of 25 students from a variety of different cultures.
>
> **Time Frame:** The explanation and activities should take no more than 30 minutes to teach.
>
> **Format:** Your lesson should include goals and objectives, materials needed, and procedures.

3. Prepositional Phrase Specifiers

Which do you think is further?

3. Prepositions

- The woman is far down the road.
- The woman is way down the road.

Why?
Which do you think is nearer?

- Larry lives just around the corner.
- Larry lives right around the corner.

Why?
Which do you think is sooner?

- Jenny turned in the test right after the bell rang.
- Jenny turned in the test just after the bell rang.

Why?
What factors account for the differences in perspective between just and right, far and way? What does this indicate about the difficulty of teaching prepositions? How can these difficulties be resolved in the ESL classroom?

4
The Subjunctive: If I Were a Rich Man

THE QUESTION

The problem with the subjunctive, interestingly, is not one most of my non-native speakers have a great deal of difficulty with. Either their languages have a comprehensive, fully-fleshed out set of subjunctive forms and established contexts in which these forms are used (be they French-speaking, Spanish-speaking or Portuguese-speaking students), or the students come from such high context cultures that context will always determine the strength of the potential. So they do not need to worry with a subjunctive at all. For my non-native speakers it is refreshingly never a serious problem. They go on about their daily lives subjunctively as if there were no other way to be. What is frequently curious to these speakers of languages where the subjunctive is fleshed out, especially Spanish speakers, is why speakers of English who find themselves in the role of learners of Spanish have so much trouble with the subjunctive. In fact, my native Spanish speakers are often queried about the ins and outs of the subjunctive as if it were an undecipherable mystery, so often so that they present the problem at English Table. "Why do English speakers have such difficulty with the subjunctive?" they ask with some surprise.

I ask back, "Well, what is the subjunctive in Spanish? What does it mean to you?"

To which they answer with a thorough but typically grammatical definition.

"No," I say, "What *is* the subjunctive? How does it function in your culture? How are you subjunctive?"

"Hmm, you know, dreaming the impossible or not so possible," they'll say.

"Do you dream a lot?" I ask.
"Oh yes, we have to. Life is too hard not to."
"Then the subjunctive is a state of mind?" I ask.
"Sure."

I am not sure at this point if it is an affirmation that life really does demand dreams, and that being subjunctive is as important as using the subjunctive, or if they simply want to move on to other subjects.

SUFFICE IT TO SAY

The *American Heritage Book of English Usage*, a helpful online e-tome which defines in some detail traditional rules of English grammar, points out that the subjunctive "is used chiefly to express the speaker's attitude about the likelihood or factuality of a given situation." It goes on to say, "English has had a subjunctive since Old English times, but most functions of the old subjunctive have been taken over by auxiliary verbs like *may* and *should*." In other words, it is not used much anymore except in some conditional clauses which will be discussed later and in such frozen expressions as, "God help me/you/him or her," "be that as it may," "come what may," and "suffice it to say." The British, further, shift into the subjunctive when they ask God to save their monarch. While it is true that the use of the subjunctive in modern English is limited, I would suggest that it remains an important component of the grammatical repertoire, especially when dreaming or giving friendly advice. Further, in keeping with the theme of **Negotiated Perspective**, the subjunctive reflects important aspects of culture, namely values of being vs. doing, the value of fate vs. achievement.[1]

THINKING SUBJUNCTIVELY

I often ask my native English-speaking students what is their greatest obstacle in the languages they are studying (usually Spanish with a little French, German, Chinese and Japanese thrown in). Almost invariably they will come back with the subjunctive (that is, except those taking Chinese and Japanese, where orthography tends to leave them thoroughly stumped). Why? I ask. Almost invariably they indicate that they do not know what it means. Rarely do they have a problem with where it goes or using it with frozen expressions such as "Ojala que...," etc. They simply do not know what it means. Better put, they do not know what it means to "be subjunctive."

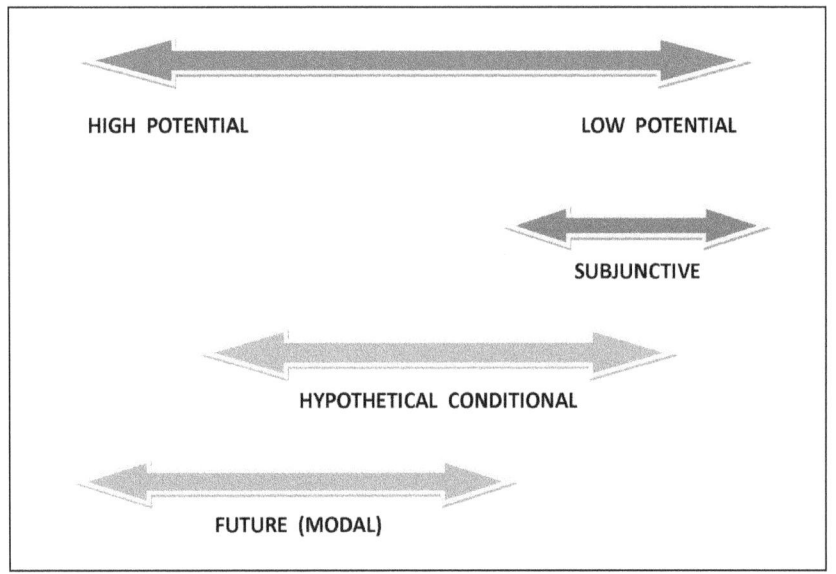

Figure 11: Subjunctive Potentiality Scale. Potentiality range from high to low potential. The lower the potential, the more likely the subjunctive will be used. The higher the potential, the more likely the future will be used. Hypothetical conditionals are mid-range. The three scales of potentiality overlap and their limits are fluid.

The subjunctive reflects a frame of mind, a way of viewing the world. Further, the subjunctive is a non-binary scalar way of thinking/dreaming falling somewhere in the neighborhood of having low potential of being fact or coming to fruition along the continuum of "likely to happen" to "never in a million years." Figure 7 above illustrates the scalar quality of potentiality. On one side are situations which have a good chance of happening. Note, however, that these are situations which have not yet occurred (if they had, they would be marked in language with the indicative mood, carrying the past or present tense). If a situation is likely to come about, speakers will commonly use the simple future, as in "I will go to the Pearl Jam concert at the end of this month." There is little doubt about your intention to attend barring some catastrophic event like a flood or fire, or barring some event, physical or mental, that suddenly makes you despise Pearl Jam.

On the other side of the scale are events or situations that have no chance of happening, and may even be viewed in the realm of pure fantasy. An example of this would be something like, "If I were the king of France, I would live on Guadeloupe year-round." This example engages in a flight of the imagination. First, last time I checked, France did not have a king or queen, and if they did it would not be me because I am not French and I would have a difficult time communicating with my subjects given that my French is limited to singing several selections from the cult-classic operetta/musical, *Les Parapluies de Cherbourg*. Second, for the reasons stated above, I have no chance of becoming king of France anytime in this lifetime. And third, since I cannot be the king of France, that pretty much rules out living in Guadeloupe (although living in Guadeloupe is more likely than becoming the king of France). The subjunctive falls at the far end of "never in a million years" side of the continuum.

What is important about the potentiality continuum is the fact that the boundaries between where the subjunctive ends and the conditional begins, or where the conditional ends and the future begins, are fluid and vary with individuals and contexts. Since the use of a modal, hypothetical conditional and/or subjunctive is so open to interpretation, context is often necessary to disambiguate meaning except, of course, in those cases wherein the entire culture agrees that an event will never happen, and the event is coded with a subjunctive phrase, as in the Spanish, *Ojala que*.... In other words, context enlightens the participants in a conversation to the certainty of the condition. As in "If I were the king of France, I would live in Guadeloupe year-round," friends or acquaintances to whom I happen to say this would know that, while I dream of living in the Caribbean, it will not happen. Yet they know I am very likely to go see Pearl Jam.

The Two Subjunctives

To Dream the Impossible Dream

The most common form of the subjunctive is the "dream statement" conditional "If I were..., I would..." ("If I had been..., I would have..."—past perfect, modal perfect). This can be illustrated with two examples of the "dream statement" subjunctive. While these two examples are identical in grammatical form, they are far different in both intention and meaning.

The first is that famous line from Tevye the Milkman's song, "If I Were a Rich Man," from *Fiddler on the Roof*. In the scene where Tevye sings "If I were a rich man," he is dreaming of a better life beyond the small, poor Jewish community of Anatevka. For the length of the song, he journeys to a dream world where abundance is a reality, where he can. All the while Tevye's reality is quite the opposite. It is only by means of a mind's-eye journey that wealth and status and privilege can be achieved. Tevye's "if I were a rich man" world view is highly subjunctive with no real potential of this dream being fulfilled. He exists intimately aware of his lot in life. His "fate" is to live out his days as a poor milkman in a poor town in a poor country. His best hopes lie with the skill of the matchmaker to find prosperous husbands for his daughters. But, alas, he knows that too is a far distant hope. For Tevye, the need to dream of a better world is borne into the very social hierarchy of his community and of the larger culture. It is his fate that his status is as a poor milkman. From that status, there is no escape. What remains are dreams.

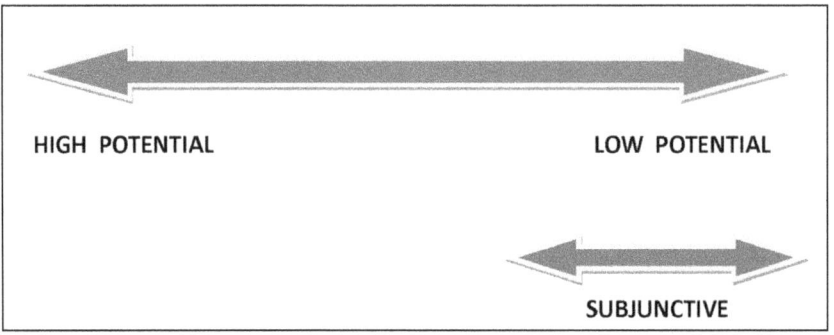

Figure 12: Tevye's Potentiality Scale: "If I *were* a rich man." The possibility of Tevye the milkman becoming a rich man is shown by the arrow on the right, extremely low given his situation in life. Of course, in the end, Tevye realizes that being "rich" has more to do with happiness than wealth. Therefore, by the end of the movie, the arrow has shifted to the other end of the scale, highly possible, even probable.

The second illustration is from a conversation a colleague of mine related to me. My colleague was out shopping for clothes with a friend. My colleague's friend found an elegant albeit expensive dress that she instantly fell in love with. Regrettably, the store did not have the dress in her size, to which the friend remarked, "If I were 20 pounds lighter, I would buy that dress."

As was the case of Tevye the milkman's world, the shopper finds herself in dream speech. She is not 20 pounds lighter and so the dress remains on the rack. Contrary to Tevye's world, however, the shopper is open to the possibility of buying the dress; the purchase can happen, but not today, not until the 20 pounds are shed. The shopper exists subjunctively in that moment. She likely realizes that the dress will probably not be there in the 10 or so weeks it takes to shed 20 pounds. She will only buy the dress when the weight is lost. For the shopper, buying the dress now does not serve as an incentive to lose weight, but as a reward for having met her weight-loss goal. She knows she is not 20 pounds lighter now, but there is potential that it will happen, although the outcome is still in doubt, as is the presence of the dress at the store. Our shopper's use of the subjunctive denotes delayed fulfillment which is not an impossibility, illustrated as follows.

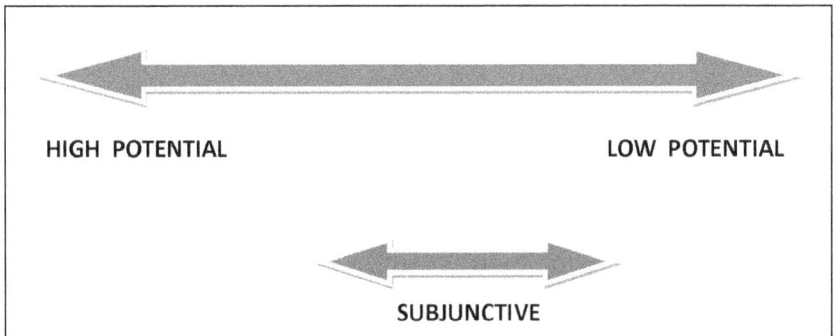

Figure 13: Shopper's Potentiality Scale. The shopper's dream world and the possibility of fulfillment. Losing twenty pounds and buying that new dress is more probable than Tevye's becoming a millionaire.

Two identical subjunctive forms, two different meanings, two different cultures.

To better understand the part culture plays in the subjunctive, I consulted a distinguished colleague, Dr. Ramon Solis, who is an accomplished Spanish novelist and poet as well as a philosopher and theologian, a colleague noted for unlocking linguistic doors seemingly impossible to open. Professor Solis spoke about the subjunctive as it is reflected in much of the Spanish-speaking world. For Professor Solis, the subjunctive reflects the plight of a people who are guided by a strong sense of faith on the one hand and a strong sense of fate on the other. When they find themselves in difficult life situations, they often chalk their state of affairs up to the inevitability of life. They are fated to be in such situations, and there is little one can do to pull oneself out of the situation, good or bad. Often, the view of life is pessimistic; life is difficult with few real options save the ones that are currently on your plate.

But there are dreams and hopes! In fact, dreams and hopes are what make life tolerable. Mind you, these dreams and hopes do not often have much of a chance of coming to fruition; they will not suddenly be realized if one just works hard enough or prays hard enough or dreams hard enough. But they are a necessary part of life, necessary to make life manageable.

By this time, Dr. Solis has my rapt attention as he deftly paints a moving portrait of the Spanish-speaking world. He ends by saying, "Spaniards never give up these dreams. They are lifelong. One reason American students find it so hard to understand the subjunctive is that they rarely have to live in the subjunctive world." Suddenly, it made sense.

Worldview is the key; a worldview that perceives one's condition in life as somehow preordained, in stark contrast to a culture rooted in achievement, where one's actions can change one's lot in life. They may even change the course of human history. Generally, the culture of the United States is driven by a strong sense that whatever one does will make a difference even if that difference is small. A person may find him or herself in a difficult situation. He or she may even perceive life as being difficult to the point of being unbearable. But these situations, good and bad, are often viewed as being transient — there is almost always a way out! So dreams carry with them a sense of potential ("anything can happen") if one works hard enough or if one puts in enough effort. It is no accident, or at least it can be conjectured that it is no accident, that the subjunctive form in English is not as fully fleshed out as it is in Spanish. There are only a few occasions when English speakers really need it, like when one wants to "dream the impossible dream."

A Bit of Friendly Advice

If you are like me, sometime in your life, your mother has said the following: "If I were you, I'd...." (In my dialect, it is sometimes intoned, "If I was you, I'd..." or "If I's you, I'd....") This form of the subjunctive in no way bespeaks of dreams, hopes and wishes. Rather, this subjunctive means business, and there are consequences for not heeding the word. The subjunctive part lies in the speaker's admitting "I am not you so I cannot overtly step into your shoes and take the action that you need to take. I can command, wheedle, or cajole you, but I cannot be you. But, I am your mother, so I sure can make strong suggestions!" The real beauty of the subjunctive here (and how mothers are so adept at this is the thing of miracles) is that the speaker is removing him or herself from making the decision of actually carrying out the "I'd" part of the suggestion, thereby assuming no responsibility whatsoever for the consequences that will surely follow if the what-comes-after-the-I'd is not fulfilled.

This form of the subjunctive is the most commonly used in English. It consists of parental advice/suggestion or friendly but strong advice from friends or teachers. Unlike dream-speech subjunctives, advice subjunctives carry high potential of fulfillment on the part of the hearer, and low potential of responsibility on the part of the speaker. The negotiated perspective.

THE NOT-SO-FINAL WORDS ON SUBJUNCTIVES

Subjunctives, like almost all grammatical forms, reflect perspective, a state of being. And like almost all grammatical features, subjunctives are scalar reflecting degrees of potentiality. In sum, the degree to which someone *is* subjunctive depends upon intention and the strength of potentiality. As one moves down the scale toward high potential, the less likely it becomes one that will use a subjunctive. But where subjunctivity begins and conditionality or modality end is a matter of speculation and debate. It could well be that the boundaries of conditionality are defined and negotiated strictly through the "eyes of the beholders" in context.

NOW YOU TRY IT!

1. Conditionality

Consider the following sentences:
- If I have the money, I will take a vacation.
- If I had the money, I would take a vacation.
- If I were to have the money, I would take a vacation.
- If I should happen to have the money, I would take a vacation.
- If I had had the money, I would have taken a vacation.

In what contexts would you use these sentences? How does verb tense influence your interpretation of these sentences?

2. Are You Going or Not?

Hwang (1979) reports that seven basic discourse types of conditionals are used two-thirds of the time in speaking and writing.[2] The most frequent form is "If + present, present," followed by "If + present, will/be going to." In fifth place is the form "If + were to/should, would/could/might." Given the contexts below, your task is to test the frequency of the following forms:
- If it rains tomorrow, I'll stay home.
- If it should rain tomorrow, I might stay home.
- If it were to rain tomorrow, I may stay home.

Context 1: You have planned for a month to go to Craggy Gardens and have a picnic with your friends. You have been looking forward to the trip for a month now. The night before, you watch the evening news. The weather reporter is predicting a 40 percent chance of showers in the mountains. Your friend calls to see if you are still interested in going to Craggy. Of the three sentences above, which are you most likely to say in the situation?

Context 2: You have been invited to go to Craggy Gardens with friends. You agree to go but you would rather spend the time on a couple pressing projects for class. In fact, as the time approaches, you grow more nervous, thinking those projects will be due soon and you don't have a lot of time to do them. The evening before the trip, you watch the evening news. The weather reporter is predicting a 40% chance of showers in the mountains. Your friend calls to see if you are still interested in going to Craggy. Of the three sentences above, which are you most likely to say in the situation?

Interview at least five people. Ask each respondent why he or she would prefer one over the other. What factors do you believe influenced respondent choice?

3. *Teaching Conditionals*

Given the Negotiated Perspective approach for explaining how conditionals function in common-usage discourse, how would you teach them given the particular students you are currently teaching? What unique and creative strategies would you employ to enable your students to understand how conditionals are understood, processed and used by native speakers of English?

5
Gerunds and Infinitives: Remembering Loving Camping

The Question

A comment made and a question asked by one of my Japanese students in class one day almost single-handedly focused my attention on a subject about which I had rarely thought, the difference between gerunds and infinitives. Gerunds, infinitives and participles (called complements in the grammar world) rarely cause the grammar world to shudder and shake by any stretch of the imagination. Verb tenses do; prepositions do; questions, commands and negatives do; even articles do; but few grammarians sit around all day and ponder why someone says "I like camping in the mountains" rather than "I like to camp in the mountains." If they do, they have too much time on their hands, and need to get some semblance of a life.

Gerunds and infinitives are small to middle-sized problems, big enough that they can cause problems from time to time, but rarely causing a ripple in the stream of conversational meaning. So, why devote a whole chapter to them? Well, the short answer is that on a March day in 1993, the curious student from Japan convinced me that the subject was worth at least pondering, if for no other reason than that gerunds and infinitives are so darned interesting, and because there actually *is* a difference between "I like camping in the mountains and "I like to camp in the mountains." Most native speakers will tell you that. But they cannot elucidate why they are different.

I do not especially remember the class that March day in 1993, but I do remember the class got off on a discussion of activities the students enjoyed doing on a regular basis. One of my three Japanese students took the floor and recited a short list of her "favorite things," swimming, cooking, playing tennis, as I recall. But what she said before reciting the list jump-started me from my after-lunch lethargy (what my medical friends call "a postprandial dip"), and launched me down a long reflective path that I am, in a sense, still on. Here's what she said:

"I enjoy to swim, to cook, and to play tennis."

"Hmm! You enjoy swimming, cooking and playing tennis," I responded uncritically, remembering the creative techniques of modeling the appropriate responses I learned from those seemingly unending hours in methods classes.

"Yes, I enjoy to do all of those things."

"*Doing* all of those things."

"Yes I do! But, Professor, why can't I say 'to do?' Isn't 'enjoy' like 'like?' I can say 'I like to swim,' right? So why not, 'I enjoy to do...'"

This student was not shy. She knew just the question to ask.

"Yes, but..."

I knew at that moment that I should have not let the student wander into this territory and that I should have left well enough alone. And I found myself up the proverbial grammar stream without a means to locomote myself back to shore, blabbering endlessly on about **the Bolinger Principle**, which I will talk about later, and only serving to get the students more and more confused.[1]

But later, this student's query got me to thinking. Well, why can't you say, "I enjoy to swim?" I know, it sounds dreadful, but there must be a reason it sounds so dreadful. And as I delved deeper into the whys of gerunds and infinitives, I discovered that these seemingly uncomplicated verbal forms have everything to do with **Negotiated Perspective**.

The Zen of Gerunds and Infinitives

There were once three Zen masters who came together for a chat. Coming upon a tub filled with clean water, one proclaimed poetically, "There is moonlight in clean water." Another protested, saying, "There is no moonlight in clean water." The third kicked over the tub.

Definitions

Leave the Zen koan hanging for just a little while. A definition of gerunds and infinitives is called for first, because most people haven't thought about these grammatical forms since they were in, say, the eighth grade, and their teacher either made them uselessly memorize a bunch of very useful verbs — some of which take gerunds, some of which take infinitives,

5. Gerunds and Infinitives

and some of which take both — or left well enough alone and simply said that gerunds are verbal nouns which end in -ing. Most people have probably forgotten all that, and with good reason.

The skinny on gerunds and infinitives is really quite simple. They do indeed function as verbal nouns, as in "*Swimming* can be beneficial to your health," or "When I was in the Museum of Modern Art, I stopped *to look* at a painting by Jasper Johns." No problem there. But they also do some really strange things, like change the meaning of a sentence depending upon which form you use. Here are two examples.

I Stopped to Look at the Painting

Go back for a moment to the Museum of Modern Art, or MOMA as it is affectionately called. You are wandering through the museum about an hour or so before closing, and a painting by Piet Mondrian jumps out at you. You are immediately struck by the painting's composition, its vibrant colors, its texture. And you stop, dead in your tracks, in front of the painting to ponder, to muse, to just take in this piece of visual magic. Not only are you appreciating good art, and paintings by Mondrian can be considered great art, but you have also been infinitival at the same time: you stopped *to look* at the painting. The "stopping" occurs first, followed by the "looking."

I Stopped Looking at the Painting

Now let's suppose that the Mondrian has so captivated you that you keep looking at the painting well after closing time. One of the guards comes up to you and says, "Hey, Bub, it's closing time. Time to quit staring at that painting." At once your thoughts shift from whatever reveries were created by Mondrian to bringing yourself back to earth and real life and out of the museum, and you leave full of joy at the time you spent enraptured by great art. In addition to being enraptured, you were gerundive: you stopped *looking* at the painting.

You stopped *to look* at the painting, and you stopped *looking* at the painting. See the difference? Arrival, departure; beginning and ending. There are scores of these kinds of sentences, where using the infinitive means something different from using the gerund.

I Remembered Turning Off the Iron

Here is another example. You have decided to go to Disney World for that dream vacation. There you are with the kids and a week's worth of stuff piled in the back of the SUV. You're an hour into the journey, and, all of a sudden, you get this sinking feeling: "Did I turn off the iron before we left?" We've all been there, haven't we? And so you mentally trace your day from waking up with your six-year-old on your stomach singing "It's a Small World After All" at the top of his little lungs, to getting in the car to leave. You go through all the steps, "Let's see now, I..., then I..., then I...," and suddenly, you remember. And you shout out loud, "Aha!!," which prompts your spouse to ask, "Aha!! What?" "I remembered *turning off* the iron before I left." "Good, don't want the house to burn down." The key here is that the remembering occurred *after* the turning off.

I Remembered to Turn Off the Iron

Same story, a bit different scene. You have decided to go to Disney World for vacation. You, the kids and a week's worth of stuff are piled in the SUV. You're an hour into the journey, and this time it's your spouse who gets the sinking feeling that somehow the iron was left on. And so he or she mentally traces the day from the "It's a Small World After All" wake-up call to getting in the car to leave. Darn it! Just can't remember. "Let's see now, I..., then I..., then I..."—still can't remember. So, outside of Brunswick, your spouse asks, "Did you remember *to turn off* the iron?" You reply, "Yes, I remembered *to turn off* the iron before we left." "Good, don't want the house to burn down." Back to Steppenwolf, "I Like to dream, yeah, yeah...." The key here is that the remembering occurred *before* the turning off.

Cases of One or the Other

Another peculiar characteristic of gerunds and infinitives is that sometimes verbs that take gerunds cannot take infinitives and vice versa. Here are two examples of this type.

The Teacher Avoided Seeing the Principal

You teach fourth grade at Pembrotanck Elementary School, and all you've heard over the past few months is the gloom and doom of the budget crisis looming over the entire state. You have read in the paper about necessary budget cuts coming down the pike. No school left behind, no teacher encouraged forward. The evening before, the school board has decided to cut one teacher from each grade at each of the schools in the district. You are diligent in your work, and believe with all your heart that you would not be the one to go. But there are lingering doubts in your mind. You decide to focus your attention on your work, toiling as diligently as ever. You make yourself as scarce as possible, fearing that if you run into the principal, she will give you the pink slip. So you avoid *seeing* the principal at all costs. You cannot avoid *to see* the principal.

Why not? As will be discovered in the following section of this discussion, gerunds and infinitives have to do, among other things, with the degree to which the speaker is emotionally attached to or involved with the action of the verb and wishes to convey this emotional attachment to the hearer; **Motivational Valence**, it was called in Chapter 1. The greater the attachment or involvement, the greater likelihood is that you will use a gerund; the greater the detachment or lack of involvement, the greater the likelihood that you will use an infinitive. In the case of "avoid seeing the principal," you may not physically catch sight of him or her. In fact, you are doing everything in your power not to run into the principal. So intent are you in your avoidance that there is no way to divest yourself of the emotional energy it takes to constantly be where the principal is not.

Sam Refuses to Admit His Failure

This example is the opposite of the one above. Sam Selleca is an aeronautical engineering whiz. He is often called upon to head up teams of troubleshooters when there is an especially difficult problem to solve or there is an important project. The army has been having trouble with one of its troop-carrying helicopters of late. Series upon series of tests have been run, but no one can figure out what is wrong with the craft. So the army turns to Sam's aeronautical engineering firm. Sam gathers a team of specialists together and runs independent tests, but, as in earlier tests, finds no structural flaw in the design of the helicopter. Sam concludes that the problem is how they were being flown. He reports this to the army, which promptly and soundly criticizes his work. Sam, being one of the best in the business, **refuses to admit** his failure in the project.

Detachment is the key here. So sure is Sam of the results of his tests that he divests himself of any blame. He may be rather put out with the Army's criticism, but he knows he is right. So he will not put any further energy into admitting something that is not the case.

Here's the Beef!

Back in Chapter 1, this handbook made the bold claim that **discourse** is the minimal unit of language. If anything, the manner in which gerunds and infinitives function in English only serves to strengthen the case.

But before going any further to lay out this argument for why gerunds and infinitives function the way they do, here are two points which are relevant to the discussion. The first is that these types of complements are difficult for non-native speakers of English because many of languages spoken by them simply do not have gerunds. Many languages have what is equivalent to -*ing* forms, but they do not function as verbal nouns per se. Many languages simply use the infinitive form for all verbal nouns.

Second, recall the concerns about the traditional methods of teaching gerunds and infinitives and the problems they generate. Problems encountered with gerunds and infinitives hark back to that age-old perception that English grammar follows a regularized, somewhat linear pattern of rules, with the obvious exceptions, and that these rules can somehow be discerned by introducing students to a set of sentences which abide by the rules and those which do not. Students memorize long lists of verbs with gerunds, infinitives, etc. It is, after all, easier that way. That is, easier for the teacher. So after having memorized these verb lists, when the learners find themselves in a context where one of these verbs is used, all they have to do is a bit of substitution and addition, and out comes the correct forms. If it were only that easy, as witnessed in my March 1994 class.

The other problem is that there are too few good pedagogical resources which explain how and why speakers "choose" between gerunds and infinitives in real-time, real-life conversation. Barbara Robinson's *Focus* text does a credible job contextualizing gerunds and infinitives.[2] But the contexts can seem contrived. Little in the teaching activities is based on enabling students to make appropriate choices in the wide variety of situations they face daily in real-time communication. Using a text like *Focus* or any of the myriad of other grammar texts which purport to be communicative, students may indeed begin to see glimpses of moonlight in the water, to borrow from the Zen koan above. But as it happens, enlightenment comes with kicking over the bucket (thankfully not "kicking the bucket"), understanding language as both a linguistic and non-linguistic/cultural phenomenon processed and constructed in the blink of an eye. The notion of grammar is neither based on static formalisms nor upon static notions of context, e.g., "Given context x ('going to the bank,' for example), speakers will automatically produce constructions y and z because context x rarely changes." It is neither arithmetic nor formulaic. Rather, grammar is largely based on the phenomenon of discourse, speakers negotiating meaning in real-time conversation.

Now for the Zen

Probably the most famous linguist to successfully tackle the difference between gerunds and infinitives was Dwight Bolinger. Professor Bolinger developed a rubric, known as the **Bolinger Principle**, in which he suggests that gerunds represent what is "real, vivid, fulfilled," while infinitives "often express something hypothetical, future, unfulfilled." The Bolinger Principle seems to work well for a variety of verbs and is extremely useful for this discussion. Another linguist by the name of Bladon studied gerunds and infinitives with such emotive verbs as *like, love* and *hate*.[3] He came to the valuable conclusion that for emotive verbs indicating desire (as in "She *likes* to have breakfast in bed"), an infinitive is used. For verbs he classifies as "enjoyment" verbs (as in "I like camping in the mountains" vs. "I like to camp in the mountains"), the operative principle is the frequency of the enjoyment; if a person regularly goes camping and enjoys it, a gerund is used. If, on the contrary, camping is occasional, an infinitive is preferred.

While this handbook relies on the work of both linguists to aid in the understanding of how gerunds and infinitives function, neither Bolinger nor Bladon discuss those all-important adaptable contextual/cultural features which serve to assist understanding of these emotive/sympathy, aspectual, and semi-implicative verbs (emotive/sentimental verbs such as *to like*, aspectual verbs *to continue* and *to start*, and a semi-implicative verb *to try*) which display subtle differences in meaning between gerunds and infinitives. The question remains, to what extent do people rely on contextual/pragmatic information when choosing between the gerund and infinitive with verbs that allow both forms?

This text would suggest that speakers of English do, in fact, perceive — albeit without overt awareness — slight differences between gerunds and infinitives. Moreover, this perception is based less on grammatical form and more on the interlocutors' perceived understanding of the context or the discourse of the conversation.

Here is a study devised to test idea. The goal of the study was to see if in fact context and discourse were important in the choice of whether to use a gerund or infinitive.

Methodology

A research instrument was devised for the study consisting of a short four-situation survey. The verbs chosen for testing represented a cross-section of verbal types which allow both gerunds and infinitives, emotive/sentimental verbs *to like*, aspectual verbs *to continue* and *to start*, and what is called a semi-implicative verb *to try*. The survey below was developed to enable those who participated in the study not only to choose between the gerund and infinitive, but also reflect on the reasons for making their choices within a particular context. The survey also accounted for differences in dialects. In other words, the contexts and questions were generic enough to fly in any part of the country without participants asking, "What in the world does that mean?" This was done to get the widest sampling possible. A random group of 158 participants were surveyed over a seven-month period. The survey (Figure 12) is found at the end of the chapter. The questions were effective, but if it were to be repeated, an interesting addition would be to ask the participants if there is any other responses they would have given and why.

Results

Even with the limitations of the study, there were some interesting results. The gerund was preferred by a margin of over two-to-one in Situations 2 and 3, whereas the infinitive was preferred almost two-to-one in Situation 4. In Situation 1, the percentage split between those who preferred the gerund and those who preferred the infinitive was identical.

Discussion

The information (statistical and anecdotal) reveal some interesting trends which support the notion that the understanding of these forms in a larger discourse is an important determinant in the choice between the gerund and the infinitive.

In those situations where the respondents perceived a clear sense of being directly involved in the action, as in Situations 2 and 3, the gerund is widely preferred over the infinitive (chalk one up for the **Bolinger Principle**). In Situation 2, respondents indicated that they preferred the gerund *camping* because the gerund emphasizes "the moment," actually experiencing the action.

One respondent stated, "...because I'm talking about something I love to do often and this time 'camping' sounds more in the present tense." Others stated, "It sounds like I'm doing it right now," "*I love camping* is more specific to me," and "*Camping* sounds like you're already there."

For Situation 3, some participants indicated that "*Working* sounds more active — in progress," "*Working* shows progress," and "When I'm telling a

Survey Results		
Total Number of Responses	Total	158
Distribution of Responses		
Situation 1		
I continued arguing...	75	47%
I continued to argue...	74	47%
No Answer	9	6%
Situation 2		
I love camping...	118	74.7%
I love to camp...	39	24.7%
No Preference	1	.6%
Situation 3		
I began working...	110	69.6%
I began to work...	43	27.2%
No Preference	5	3.2%
Situation 4		
I've tried losing weight...	53	34%
I've tried to lose weight...	102	65%
No Preference	3	1%

Figure 14: Gerunds and Infinitives Numerical Results. The data are presented as follows: Column One — Numerical Totals; Column Two — Percentages.

Figure 15: Camping. A campsite at Price Lake on the Blue Ridge Parkway in Western North Carolina.

story, I put myself where I was. I was not *to work*, I was *working*." When the infinitive was preferred, the respondents perceived some distance in space and time between themselves and the situation. One respondent stated, "*To* indicates something you are going to do and haven't done yet or are just starting."

In Situations 2 and 3, what seems to be going on here is the respondents' perception of their personal involvement in the situation. If the respondent is able to place himself on the shore of Price Lake or in his study late at night, even though the respondent may be removed from the situation by both time and space (as in these participant interviews), the respondent will most likely choose the gerund. The respondents may not be physically there, but their minds are!

Situation 4 presents a different set of contextual and pragmatic issues. Most respondents perceived the person in the story and context as being unsuccessful in his or her attempt to lose weight. Because of this lack of success, almost twice as many respondents preferred the infinitive to the gerund.

However, when the participants had a chance to say why they chose the form they did, they revealed certain subtle psycholinguistic factors which go beyond Bolinger's description of the infinitive, which he said denoted unfulfilled or hypothetical action in time. For those who chose the infinitive, three themes seem to surface.

First, many participants indicated that using the infinitive implied that they "gave up" the diet through a conscious deliberate act. In this case, they surrendered any emotional attachment to the diet; they threw in the proverbial towel.

Second, several said that the act of dieting is a long-term on-again-off-again activity over the course of a lifetime. One respondent put it this way, "The second choice (infinitive) seems like a past gradual action. It sounds long-lasting." Another stated, "The second indicates that I want to be rid of (the weight) but I'm not now in the process of dieting." In this case, there is a sense that ultimate fulfillment is down the road — they are not living "subjunctively." They are confident they will eventually lose the weight. However, their focus is on the process of dieting rather than the end product of achieving the desired weight. So, in their answers there is a hint of delayed fulfillment, but it has not been achieved yet. So they preferred an infinitive.

The third reason given for choosing the infinitive was that many respondents indicated they would feel a sense of disappointment for having failed to meet their dieting goals. This can be seen in the response of one participant: "I always say that after I've blown a diet. It expresses that I've tried and failed or had a setback."

A few others who chose the infinitive did so for other reasons than the feeling of unfulfilled goals. One respondent said "I don't talk about my weight with anyone but close friends and family, so I'd probably be more informal." To this respondent, the infinitive seems less formal in this situation, but interestingly, she indicated that the infinitive sounds more formal in Situation 1.

Another respondent answered, "I would say #2 (infinitive) because that's what they say on all the Slim-Fast commercials (referring to the phrase in the survey, "You are a month into a new diet that has been *guaranteed to take off the weight and keep it off*").

Interestingly, among those who chose the gerund, participants responded with such answers as: "#2 sounds like I gave up, and I never give up" (emotional attachment and commitment); "The first answer seems more informal. It sounds as if the person has exerted effort" (emotional commitment and attachment); "It [the weight] is not gone yet but it will be"; and "I'm still trying." The most interesting response was: "Losing infers [*sic*] that the weight might return which is natural. *To lose* is inappropriate because it would mean it is a permanent loss, thus contradicting nature."

These responses suggest that the degree to which the person feels committed to continuing a program of weight loss or the degree to which the participant feels he or she is succeeding in the short term of his or her diet program is the primary reason for choosing the infinitive versus the gerund.

Situation 1 presents a different type of problem, one which is probably not addressed in any mainstream grammar book. The verb *continue* seems to support the use of the gerund since the reported situation involves ongoing activity. However, the results of the study show that there was an even split between those preferring the gerund and those preferring the infinitive.

The prevailing reason for this has to do with two contextual/pragmatic notions: (1) the perceived degree of the formality of the situation (i.e., the respondents would relate the situation in a different way to family members than to friends), and (2) whether or not the primary focus of the respondent is on the argument with the police officer or the retelling of the story of an argument with a police officer that happened in the past. In other words, the issue here is the extent to which the respondent is reflecting his or her emotional distance, **Motivational Valence**, to or away from the event.

The respondents who chose the gerund perceived the focus of the situation as directed toward the larger context of relating or retelling the story about an argument with a police officer to a friend and not about the argument with the police officer itself. Many who selected the gerund indicated that, when relating a story to a friend or a member of one's family, it was more appropriate to use a form perceived as being less formal, in this case the gerund. One respondent said, "*To argue* seems so formal when talking to a friend about what I was angry about." Another declared, "The first is slightly more informal, and so I might be more likely to use that in a conversation with a friend." Storytelling was their focus, so they wanted to create a less formal context to relate the events.

Of the respondents who chose the infinitive and indicated their reasons behind their choice, many said that the infinitive implied a higher degree of formality than the gerund. These respondents said that there is a proper procedure for arguing with a police officer, using a more formal tone, as opposed to the process of arguing with a friend, spouse or neighbor. Responses such as "sounds better, more formal with the police" were numerous among those who chose the infinitive.

Interestingly, nine respondents refused to answer the query, indicating that it is inappropriate to argue with a police officer in any circumstance. Wise choice! Some respondents even said that they would say something different altogether, like "I kept on arguing with the police officer," using a phrasal verb considered even less formal than a verbal noun, possibly as a storytelling technique.

In any case, this short study seems to support the opinion that native speakers do perceive a difference in meaning when a gerund is used and when an infinitive is used, although they may not by totally aware of it unless asked to reflect on their reasons (and even then they may not totally aware of their reasons). Moreover, the study indicates that this scalar notion of emotional involvement and attachment, or lack thereof, is perhaps the defining criterion in the choice of a gerund or an infinitive in a discourse. What is more, the oral responses of the participants said much about who they are and how they perceive the world, even if their reasons for choosing gerunds and infinitives remain hidden.

THE UNUSUAL CASE OF LIKE AND ENJOY

There remains, however, one proverbial "fly in the ointment" in the discussion of gerunds and infinitives: the case of *like*, *love*, *hate* and their associated verbs.

Consider the case of *like* and *enjoy* as they apply to the usage of gerunds and infinitives. *Love* and *hate* and the associated verb, *like*, represent a very interesting paradox in terms of gerund and infinitive usage. For example, *love*, *like* and *hate* can all take both the gerund and infinitive, and carry much the same meaning no matter which form is used, i.e.:

> I love to go to the movies on Saturday.
> I love going to the movies on Saturday.
> I hate to go to the movies on Saturday.
> I hate going to the movies on Saturday.
> I like to go to the movies on Saturday.
> I like going to the movies on Saturday.

What about emotive verbs associated with *love*, *like* and *hate*, verbs such as *enjoy*, *adore*, *abhor* and *detest*? Logically, since *love* or *like* and *enjoy* belong to the same general class of verbs, it should be quite acceptable to say, "I enjoy to go to the movies on Saturday." But in fact, "I enjoy to go to the movies" is an ill-formed construction for reasons which are not solely based on syntax. In fact, the associative verb can only take gerundive forms. To use an infinitive would render the sentence ungrammatical. These associated verbs are:

Love Verbs	**Hate Verbs**
enjoy	abhor
fancy	detest
adore	despise

WHY?

To answer this question, it is necessary to make another very important point about grammar, any grammar. It is a point made in the introduction. Grammar is not binary, that is, it is not either this or that. For instance, one can understand words as being particular parts of speech. Take the word *by*. In binary terms, one could well define *by* as a preposition. And that would be right. But *by*, added to a word or two, could just as well function as an adverb, as in "I had to go downtown this morning. My car was in the shop so I had to go by bus," or a logical connector, called a conjunction in a former life, as in "By and by, the construction crew came out and fixed my roof like they said they were going to do." The point is grammar is scalar, gradable, on a continuum.

This scalar view of grammar aids understanding of the *like* and *enjoy* conundrum. Verbs such as *like*, *love* and *hate* have a wide range of meanings and emotions associated with these meanings. In other words, you can like, love or hate someone or something strongly or weakly or somewhere in between. The now famous beer commercial which featured a love-struck man professing his love to another man by saying, "I love you, man," was effective because of its use of irony. The professor (the one who professes) did not really love the professee in the devotional sense. Actually the professor simply wanted the other guy's beer. Likewise, in the movie *Green Card*, the character played by Andie MacDowell acknowledged that she "hated" the character played by Gerard Depardieu, when she actually loved him.

But the associative verbs are different. Their range of meanings and associated emotions is much narrower to the extent that it is difficult not to experience the emotion associated with the verb. It is difficult to abhor something and not experience the fullness of the emotion that goes with abhorrence. As one of my students commented on one occasion, "Think of it as putting a large Coke cup inside a biggie Coke cup. 'Like' is the biggie cup and 'enjoy' the large cup. In other words, I like everything I enjoy but I don't enjoy everything I like. I like exercising — I like what it does for my health, but I often don't enjoy it, especially when I force myself to get up at six in the morning to run."

While many linguists have sought to answer this dilemma by looking at the history and semantics of this class or classes of verbs, and while many of these solutions may be quite valid, even elegant, the student's reply above gives us a useful straightforward rubric to explain this problem to our non-native speaker students.

Conclusion

In summary, attempts at explaining the usage of gerunds and infinitives on syntactic and semantic grounds alone have met with limited success. If these paradigms do not work, then what motivates the choice of the gerundive form over the infinitive and vice versa? The choice between the gerund and the infinitive is quite complex, often motivated by a number of pragmatic and discoursal factors. An interlocutor's understanding of an event and his or her role in it is often the primary motivating factor for grammatical choice. Unfortunately, contextual/pragmatic dynamics are often open and non-linear, thus difficult to predict, much less codify. However, as has been demonstrated above, a few preliminary assumptions can be reached in regard to the choice of a gerund versus an infinitive. Among these are: one, the interlocutor's sense of immediacy with regard to the event (that is, in relating an event, to what extent does the interlocutor place him or

5. Gerunds and Infinitives

herself in the time and place of the event?); two, the degree of perceived formality of a situation; and three, the degree to which a person is personally affected or not affected by the situation.

As speakers negotiate meaning by enabling their hearers to understand their perspectives, grammatical choice — in this case, the choice between

---

Participant Survey

In what place have you lived the longest?
Where do you live now?
Do you think you talk like most of the people in your hometown? Why or why not?
Please read the situations below. Indicate the phrase you might use. Then indicate why you chose your answer. There are no right or wrong answers.

Situation 1:
On your way home from work, a police officer pulls you over and claims you were speeding. Angered by the inconvenience, you insist that you were not speeding, but the officer tickets you anyway. As you are relating this event to a friend,
Which are you more likely to say?
(1) I continued arguing with the police officer but I didn't get anywhere.
(2) I continued to argue with the police officer but I didn't get anywhere.
Why did you make this choice?

Situation 2:
You are finally taking a much needed vacation. You are camping at Price Lake in the Blue Ridge Mountains, and you wake up on a beautiful summer morning to the sounds of the birds singing. You are ecstatic to be in the mountains away from work and the phone. As you watch the mist rising over the lake, which are you more likely to say?
(1) I love camping in the mountains!
(2) I love to camp in the mountains!
Why did you make this choice?

Situation 3:
Your boss has given you until Friday to complete a major project at work. If you are successful, you are in line for a sizable promotion and raise. It is the Wednesday before the project is due, and the project is not falling into place. Finally, early Thursday morning you had a brainstorm and began the project. At work on Thursday, you are tired but relieved that the project is going well. You relate this to one of your colleagues.
Which are you more likely to say?
(1) I began working on the project at 3 this morning.
(2) I began to work on the project at 3 this morning.
Why did you make this choice?

Situation 4:
You are frustrated! Very frustrated!! You are a month into a new diet that has been guaranteed to take off the weight and keep it off. But it isn't working. You are talking to a friend about your frustration.
Which are you more likely to say?
(1) I've tried losing weight, but I just can't seem to!
(2) I've tried to lose weight, but I just can't seem to!
Why did you make this choice?

Figure 16: The Study Survey — Gerunds and Infinitives. Questions and options given orally to 158 respondents over the period of six months.

gerunds and infinitives — depends greatly upon the situation and how the speaker and listener perceive it. Often subtle pragmatic factors, such as the degree of affectedness or degree of formality, are the main determinants for choosing one grammatical form over another. How these factors are considered in the development of instructional activities in the ESL classroom will greatly determine how successful students are in acquiring the gerund and infinitive. Teaching grammar in general, and gerunds and infinitives specifically, becomes the project of engagement, intentionally enabling students to reach the proverbial fork in the road in order that they might understand, and in some sense, create a new reality based on the **Negotiated Perspective** of discourse.

Now You Try It!

Teaching Gerunds and Infinitives

Given the Negotiated Perspective approach for explaining how gerunds and infinitives function in common-usage discourse, how would you teach them to the particular students you are currently teaching? What unique and creative strategies would you employ to enable your students to understand how gerunds and infinitives are understood, processed and used by native speakers of English?

6
Verbs: Come Together

THE QUESTION

It's not so much a question as an answer that motivates this discussion. On the first day of every semester, I discover from my international students what gives them the most trouble in English and what they would like to learn. Usually, these two correspond, and more often than not, revolve around grammatical subjects. The issue that seems to give them the most headaches is the verb.

And it is put that simply: "We want to know more about the verb!" Now, granted, "the verb" is a huge topic, one that would encompass more than a semester or two to discuss if one did it justice. It is of such importance that whole volumes have been written about it, whole linguistic theories have been developed around it, including generative grammar, where at one time the notions of AUX and "c-Commanding," which are mental constructs of verbness, held sway. Truly no discussion of English grammar would be complete without an examination of the verb.

For the purposes of this handbook, those purposes being how Negotiated Perspective and English common-usage grammar intersect, this text proposes a somewhat different slant on the verb. Rather than examining every single feature of tense, aspect and modality in great detail, it offers a unique view into the Four Perspectives of language, introduced in the Chapter 1 of this tome and discussed throughout, which encompass every detail of the verb, and perhaps, the whole grammatical system of English.

THE FOUR PERSPECTIVES

As seen in earlier discussions, the issue of using language to communicate identifiable and coherent messages is multifaceted. Speakers have access to a myriad of linguistic devices designed to help the person with whom they are speaking understand what is being expressed, all within the scope of discourse. While discourse is the central coherent unit of language, it is the verb that enables discourse to be coherent and to flow. The verb is central to the understanding of perspective. The verb carries perspective in terms of event structure, interconnecting the many facets of discourse.

Over the course of this handbook, the efficacy of the Mascagni Effect and its many components — including the Four Perspectives — has been demonstrated. The uniqueness of the verb lies in the fact that all verbs carry varying degrees of all four perspectives. The discussion in the subsequent three chapters revolves around how the Four Perspectives and the verb interface.

7
Negatives, Interrogatives and Imperatives: Don't Ask and Don't Tell (Manipulative Speech Acts)

THE QUESTION

When she stepped off the US Airways 757 at the Charlotte-Douglas International Airport, the final stop in a two-day, three-city adventure, Kyoko Yamashita's dream of coming to the United States to study English had finally been realized. And she was excited. Every day for almost five years, Kyoko practiced English, with her teachers, with her friends, in front of the mirror. She watched Disney movies, Steven Spielberg movies, Michael Crichton movies. She watched as six unlikely and ill-matched young men and women became *Friends*. She watched as a young progressive governor from New Hampshire, Jed Bartlet, became president of the United States for good and bad. She watched as teams of physicians and nurses bandaged, operated, shouted, cajoled, and healed people from all walks of life in a place called *ER*. For five years, Kyoko thought American, ate American, slept American, and acted American. And now she was finally *in* America.

When Kyoko first arrived on the Appalachian State University campus for the fall semester, she was thrilled at the many new things she was experiencing. Campus life was everything she had read about: getting used to roommates, parties, professors who lectured with great enthusiasm and energy about subjects on which they were knowledgeable. Kyoko quickly settled into a comfortable routine, and life was very good. At least at first. Then, after about a month or so in her one-year tenure, things began to unravel ever so slightly. She began to be confused by the vocabulary the students were using. It seemed that just about every other word was a slang expression she had never heard before. And she was confused by the accents. While she had watched a lot of American TV, she found herself ill-prepared to understand the varieties of Southern accents she found on campus and in the community.

The straw that broke the camel's back and prompted Kyoko to come to my office for a serious discussion of dialect and culture shock was an incident that happened to her with a family she had met at one of the local churches. It seems that Kyoko had gone to visit one of the local churches with a friend of hers, and a family in the church, locals from Watauga County, invited Kyoko and her friend for a picnic on the Blue Ridge Parkway. Kyoko described the picnic as mostly fun, but the accents were hard to understand, very hard. But it was an incident at day's end that had Kyoko confused and telling me that people in this region sure talk funny. As the family was packing up to leave, the father said, "Well, let's go to the house!"

"I'm sorry," Kyoko said, "I can't go with you. I have to go study for a test."

"Excuse me?" the father replied.

"I can't go to the house with you. I have to study for a test in my history class tomorrow." To which the father chuckled. "Oh no, I'm not inviting you. This is just our way to say goodbye."

Speech Acts

Philosopher J.L. Austin was the first to coin the term **Speech Act**. According to Austin, a speech act comprises a "language performance," a particular discourse used to "do" something in a particular context. He contends that any time language is used, whether in spoken or written form (and probably signed form, as well), interlocutors are "doing something" linguistically. Austin points to three types of speech acts.[1]

The first he terms **locutionary**, that is, "saying something." When humans enter into conversation, they utilize language for the purpose of communication. One could even extend Austin's definition a bit further to say that when a person talks to him or herself, that speech act is also locutionary in that the desired intention is to "say something" even if the speaker and hearer are the same.

The second type of speech act Austin terms **illocutionary**. An illocutionary speech act is one in which an act is accomplished *in* saying something. Say, for example, you are teaching a grammar class in Boone, North Carolina, in February. Now imagine that an unusual break in the winter weather has occurred, and the temperature outside is hovering at an almost balmy 50 degrees Fahrenheit. But February in Boone is usually bitterly cold, so the heat is still on full blast in the building, and, as a result, you are sweating profusely and the students are about to pass out from the heat. Now instead of directly asking the students at the back of the room to get up and open the windows, you utter the following: "Gee, don't you think it's hot in here?" At this point, the students at the back of the room "get the hint" and open the windows. What you have done is illocutionary, that is, *in* saying "Don't you think it's hot in here?," something happens, not merely by saying the words, but by an action which follows the words. One could well argue — correctly, by the way — that any command, or any question for that matter, is illocutionary, that is, something happens, or is supposed to happen, after the command has been given or the question asked.

The third type of speech act, according to Austin, is **perlocutionary**. By perlocutionary, Austin means that an act is completed *by* saying something. Austin sees an important distinction between *in* and *by*, one which Austin does not make altogether convincingly. Think of it this way. You are getting married. You have planned the wedding for almost a year. You've ordered the flowers, the caterer, the dress, the tuxedos, the church or synagogue or mosque and the minister, rabbi, or imam, and you've paid your first installment of the whopping $65,000 for everything. So the wedding day arrives, and you stand at the front of the place of worship. You answer questions, exchange vows, swap rings. Then, after all is said and done, the officiant utters the following words: "By the power vested in me by the State of North Carolina and by whatever faith it happens to be, I now pronounce you husband and wife." At that moment, and only at that moment, you are officially married. In other words, the act of saying the words performs the marriage! Incidentally, you can do without everything else in a wedding. You do not need the caterer, the flowers, the bridesmaids or groomsmen. You do, however, need the words "By the power vested in me by the State of North Carolina and by whatever faith it happens to be, I now pronounce you husband and wife," and, of course, the signed marriage license which is recorded at the county courthouse.

Austin's Speech Act theory was taken up by philosopher John Searle. Like Austin, Searle views speech acts expansively because one can do many things with language.[2] One can describe, explain, persuade, command, question, negate, and perform. Likewise, one can foreground, background, focus, and interact with language. Searle views speech acts as a function of communication, or as Honderich describes Searle's theory, "Illocution is a function of unformalized circumstances."[3]

Austin and Searle's expansive definition of **speech act** has a lot of merit, and adds insight to how language functions in communication. For this discussion, the focus will revolve around one particular type of speech act, **manipulation**. Manipulative speech acts, as far as linguists can tell, come in three flavors — negatives, interrogatives and imperatives — all of which have as their goal to change the status quo. How they go about it is fascinating and has everything to do with perspective.

TO BE OR NOT TO BE, THAT REALLY IS THE QUESTION

As discovered throughout the discussion in this book, culture plays a tremendously important role in day-to-day interactions. Culture, however it is defined by a particular speech community, establishes values and norms of behavior. And while cultures modify their norms over time, members of a society do not always conform inestimably to these values and behaviors all the time. There are, after all, revolutions and protests big and small. And on any given day, probably at any given moment, there are those small protestations which do not necessarily shake the world on its foundations, but change relationships.

Here is an example. Two years ago, I went to Tokyo on business. Now, I have to tell you that I do not speak a lot of Japanese, just the necessary phrases to get by, greetings, thank yous, "Where is...?" and "How much?" questions. And even my "Where is...?" questioning is weak because, after I ask "Where is...?" in Japanese, invariably, the askee will respond in Japanese, and I usually do not have the slightest idea what he or she is saying unless he or she points, and then I simply follow the direction of the point. I then must resort to asking someone else, and usually the direction of the point changes and I turn. I can typically get to my destination, but I almost always walk because the thought of the language needed to negotiate a taxi overwhelms me.

At any rate, one day while I was there I needed to get across the city quickly, and a taxi was my best alternative. So, for about two hours, I studied the questions I needed to ask the driver, and I studied every possible response I could think of, which, incidentally, is not a good way to learn a language, because people have this annoying tendency to say something you have not studied. So I went in search of a taxi, and soon found one near my hotel. And, in the best Japanese I could muster for the occasion, I asked if he could take me to where I needed to go. He acknowledged my presence politely,

7. Negatives, Interrogatives and Imperatives 113

smiled, and then made a curious sucking sound through his teeth, a sucking sound for which I was not prepared.

What does a "teeth suck" mean? I saw no "teeth suck" in my *Learn Japanese in Ten Minutes a Day* text. Puzzled, I asked again, and the response was the same sucking sound. Fortunately for me, a Japanese man who both knew his culture and my language came along and explained to me that the taxi driver could not take me to my destination because he was off duty. He directed me to another taxi, negotiated with the driver for me, and I was off. On the way to the taxi, I asked the man what the strange sucking sound meant. I had never experienced that response. Even though I had many Japanese students, there was nary a teeth sucker among them, at least not at Appalachian State University. The man explained that sucking through the teeth is a polite way to say no. "The driver did not want to offend you," the man said, "but he also did not want to drive you."

As I was being driven to my destination across Tokyo, I put two and two together and thought to myself, "Hmm, the driver was saying no in a high context way." In Japan, it is important to maintain a sense of propriety, especially to those considered *gaijin*, foreigners. To answer my inquiry with *iie*, "no," or even the more polite *iie chigai masu*, loosely translated, "I'm not able to," would be considered a social faux pas, lacking proper decorum. The driver was, to be sure, challenging my assumptions, i.e., that he was free to take me to my destination, but the challenge was rendered in a socially acceptable manner. In other words, cultures establish the means by which you say *no* to someone.

Negation serves as a linguistic means to challenge the norms of culture, or, not so insignificantly, the assumptions of a conversation. To be sure, negation can be strongly confrontational. Back during the Vietnam War and, more recently, when President Bush was considering the invasion of Iraq, there were a multitude of protests, and one of the more confrontational slogans in those remonstrations was, "Hell No, We Won't Go!" On a more mundane level, if your teenage son asks to borrow the Porsche to go out with his friends, you may respond with a strong, "No!" and nothing else, especially not the keys.

In addition to being confrontational, negation can actually be used to ameliorate potential conflict. But the amelioration is in how you say *no*. Linguist Tom Givon lists a number of these toning-down devices which, when coupled with negatives, soften the blow of the negative.[4]

To illustrate these devices, let's again say that your teenage son wants to borrow the Porsche to go out with his friends. You do not want to be overly confrontational. You and your son have been working on resolving the conflicts in your relationship. You could respond by using a modal, as in "I can't lend you the Porsche. It might be a bit too fast for your level of driving experience." You could use the subjunctive, "If I were you, I would take the Camry. It is a lot safer." You could say *no* with a conditional, "If I let you have a car tonight, it'll have to be the Camry. I'll feel better about you driving it rather than the Porsche," or with a yes/no question, which is, of course, rhetorical: "Wouldn't it be better if you took the Camry? The Porsche is a bit too fast for your level of driving experience." Finally, you could use an adverbial to soften your *no*: "I'm terribly concerned about your driving the Porsche, especially since you have just now finished your driver's ed course."

You could use one or more of these in a myriad of combinations. The son will probably be disappointed, maybe even a bit piqued, but not as mad as if you had come right out and said "No!" with no discussion.

Another technique to avoid a possible confrontation when using a negative is through clause length. You could go on and on for an hour illustrating in great detail why it is not wise to take the Porsche. As the clincher, you could even slip in the now famous and graphic movie produced by the Ohio Highway Patrol showing the potential results of taking the Porsche rather than the Camry. Of course, your son may either not drive for the next 30 years or join the NASCAR circuit.

Techniques for saying **no** are important in the maintenance of relationships. In my community, speakers who are native to the area have a curious expression which means *no* and *yes*, although not at the same time. The phrase *I don't care to* carries both connotations. Once, I went to Johnson City, Tennessee, with a friend of mine. He had to take his car in to the dealership for service. When he arrived and pulled up to one of the garages, the service manager came out and asked, "Would you care to move around to the third bay over there? We are finishing up a seminar here." My friend responded, "I don't care to," which meant, "It would be no problem whatsoever to accede to your request." He was saying *yes*. If the service manager had come out and asked him for a $1000 donation to buy a new diagnostic computer for the shop, he may have responded, "I don't care to," which would suggest that he had absolutely no interest in doling out that much cash for a diagnostic machine, even if were to be used on his car. He would be saying *no*. And the service manager would discern the difference between yes and no.

How does one tell the difference? For one thing, context will usually disambiguate the two meanings. But if one is still not sure, one needs to listen for the intonation at the end of the expression. If it rises, it means *yes*. If it falls, it means *no*.

7. Negatives, Interrogatives and Imperatives   115

To close this discussion on negation and perspective, something needs to be said about double negatives, one of the true banes of prescriptive grammarians. It is not uncommon to hear such ear-splitting discourse as, "I ain't got no money," or "Don't say nothing about this, but I heard that...," or one heard on the dialectal video *American Tongues*: "Let's don't let no stump knock no hole in this here boat."[6]

Less colloquially, one periodically hears expressions like, "I've not decided not to go," or "I'm not unhappy with you." These two examples are discoursally interesting. Neither denote their opposites. "I've not decided not to go" does not mean that I've definitely decided to go. It simply means that my mind is not made up yet. I may go and I may not. A possible discourse might go something like this:

"Rick, are you going to the Limp Bizkit concert tonight? I know this morning you were leaning toward not going. So what gives?"

"Well, I don't know. I've not decided not to go, but I haven't decided to go either. I can't make up my mind. I guess I'll decide when it's time to go. Somebody gave me these tickets, and Limp Bizkit is not my favorite band, but I don't dislike 'em either."

Likewise, the phrase, "I'm not unhappy with you," does not denote its opposite. Look at "I'm not unhappy with you" in the following discourse. Let's say that you had been looking forward to going to the Limp Bizkit concert for about three months, ever since the band announced it would make a tour stop in your town. As soon as you heard the good news about the concert, you called me up to see if I wanted to go with you. Being a Limp Bizkit fan myself, I responded that I would love to go, and asked would you buy a ticket for me. So the tickets were bought, and the excitement grew in anticipation of the concert. About four days before the concert, for no apparent reason, I began to get cold feet. I decided that Limp Bizkit was not that great a band, especially after having discovered the Dave Matthews Band. So with little explanation, I called you the day before the concert and explained that I would not be going. You were not especially happy with me at the time, and expressed a bit of anger. But you insisted that you would go by yourself if you had to. And you went, had a great time, and immediately went out and bought Limp Bizkit's new CD. We talked the day after the concert, and you told me how good the concert was. When I asked you if you were disappointed that I had not gone with you, you explained that you weren't unhappy with me, that you had a good time at the concert, but that it would have been more fun had I gone. Although you were not unhappy with me, you were not happy with me either. The feeling is not one of neutrality, but rather one of being specifically let down that I decided not to go the concert while being generally satisfied with our relationship.

What gives with double negatives? Why do they provoke such consternation, or worse, such revulsion? The answer lies in the application of Aristotelian logic to language. In this form of logic, $not(not\ P) = P$. That is, two negatives make a positive. So, applying the canon of logic, if you *ain't* (negative #1, which also causes more than its share of disgust) got *no* (negative #2) money, you actually have money. Now, the problem is that no one in his right mind would ever interpret, "I ain't got no money," to mean "I have money," unless he was trying to make a point that the speaker should be better versed in Aristotelian logic and should not be using double negatives. In anybody's book, "I ain't got no money," means the wallet or pocket is empty. The aversion to such an expression comes not from the knowledge of logic or lack of it, but from the pragmatic sense that educated people do not use such language. The truly erudite refrain from using *ain't*, giving preference to "I don't have any money," if the speaker wishes to be informal, or "I haven't any money," if the speaker wishes to be formal. Logic is not the issue here; emphasis is. The second negative serves to heighten or emphasize the first negative: "What I'm saying is true. My wallet is empty! Can *you* spare a buck or two?"

HONEY, DO YOU REALLY LOVE ME?

The process of asking questions may, at first glance, appear to be a subject that does not need a great deal of discussion. After all, is this procedure not clear-cut? You desire some information that you assume I am in possession of. So you request that I proffer this information. What is more, you assume that the information you receive will be both true and relevant to your request. Simple, right? Unfortunately, asking questions is far from simple and straightforward. For as one of my graduate students is fond of saying, it depends on why you're asking the question and who you're asking the question.

There are three predominant types of **interrogatives** (question strategies): yes/no questions, wh-questions, and tag questions. Of the three interrogative categories, wh-questions are perhaps the easiest for non-native speakers to comprehend. With these, the speaker and hearer have the same knowledge except for one or more elements signified by the wh-question word, either who, what, where, why, when and how (*how come* in my dialect). The missing element or elements become the focus of the discourse. One

7. Negatives, Interrogatives and Imperatives 117

interesting point about wh-questions is what happens to the focus of the discourse if the wh-question word is not inverted, that is, comes at the beginning. For example, "He did what?" vs. "What did he do?" In the latter, the questioner is seeking a tidbit of information. In the former, the questioner has probably been given the tidbit, but is expressing surprise about the information.

Let's return to our Limp Bizkit story. Suppose on the night of the concert (you remember, the one I did not attend even though I had a ticket), I went out with your girlfriend instead. Let's suppose someone saw us out together, and that someone related my tryst to you. Besides a few choice words interspersed into the conversation, you may have said, "He did what?" You knew what I did, but you are shocked that I did it! Other than the expression of surprise, the discoursal function of wh-questions is pretty straightforward.

This is not the case with yes/no questions. On the surface, yes/no questions appear to elicit basic information and/or opinions. "Are you Rick?" "Yes." "Have you ever been to Ulan Bator?" "No." Easy enough, but as Georgetown linguist Deborah Tannen has shown, yes/no questions are not simply about yes or no. In her interesting and widely read treatment of the differences between male and female conventions in language, *Please Understand Me*, Professor Tannen explains that men and women understand yes/no questions differently.[7] Women view yes/no questions as rarely being about factual information, but rather about relationships. Posing a yes/no question initiates some kind of negotiation. Let me illustrate this with an exaggerated example that, mind you, does not occur in my household (I have learned about these things), but, as many men and women have indicated, happens in households throughout this land of ours. You (a male) are driving along the interstate, and your wife or girlfriend asks you, "Are you hungry?" Simple yes/no question, right? You answer "No," and drive past exit 46 with the McDonald's, Chick-fil-a, and Shoney's. A few minutes later, she turns to you and says, "You know that you are very inconsiderate, don't you?"

You respond, "Huh? Where did that come from?"

"Well, a few minutes ago, I asked you if you were hungry!"

"I remember," you say, "and I said no because I'm not really hungry right now."

"That's my point. You're inconsiderate! You never asked me if I was hungry," she responds.

I will not finish the conversation because, as I said before, it is quite exaggerated. The point is, according to Tannen, that when she asked, "Are you hungry?," the question was the beginning of a negotiation, perhaps to decide when an appropriate time and place to eat might be. The question was about relationship. *He* interpreted the question as being about food and hunger. They missed each other because they misinterpreted the intention of the question. Tannen's thought-provoking conclusion is that males and females learn the function of yes/no questions in their play time. When little girls play together, they endeavor to reach consensus. So they continually negotiate with each other. Yes/no questions function as relationship checks. Boys, on the other hand, compete with each other to discover who is fastest, strongest, smartest, etc. In the quest of competition, information gathering is essential; information drives rivalry.

Sometimes yes/no questions, solely intended to elicit a yes or no answer, can be misinterpreted as another type of manipulative speech act, especially if the hearer is not familiar with the finer nuances of English idiomatic expressions. The following humorous narrative is a perfect example of this. It was related to me by my good friend Victor Pájaro, a native of Colombia, South America, and who is a very fine language student and teacher. Interestingly, this experience occurred while Victor was a beginning English student, and had very little facility with the language. Victor found himself in a training class for naval personnel. As the scenario below describes, the instructor of the course misread Victor's language level and assumed that Victor could understand some of the finer points of English:

> When Mr. David Gomez [not his real name] informed me that I had been selected to study boilers in a United States Navy school, I was thrilled to death. Little did I know that I was en route to meet head to head with perhaps the greatest experience an ESL student can go through in the process of learning the English language.
>
> I was also informed that since I had such an excellent command of the English language (about 150 words at the time), another non–English-speaking petty officer would be participating in the classes, and that I had been assigned the responsibility to translate/interpret and tutor this individual throughout the duration of the course."
>
> "It didn't take too long for us to learn the daily routine of going to classes, eating our meals, and following most of the school's policies. Basically, all we had to do was follow what the guys in our group were doing. So we practically didn't need the language. I, the one considered to be the language expert, only understood three per cent at most of what they said, so we clung to the old adage, "When in Rome...."
>
> One day, the instructor had been teaching for about 45 minutes. Suddenly, he looked directly at the location where my partner and I were sitting and said, "With the Colombians. Do you follow me?" I replied, "Yes, sir." At this point he said, "Take ten," meaning a ten-minute break. We,

Colombians, started to follow the instructor. The following oral interaction took place after the instructor discovered that we were following him:

INSTRUCTOR: "Why are you following me?"
VICTOR: "You told us in class to follow you."
INSTRUCTOR: "No! No! What I meant was, if you've got the picture."
MY PARTNER: "What is he talking about?"
VICTOR: "Creo que debemos ir a algún lugar para que nos tamen una foto." (I think we have to go somewhere and have a picture taken.)
VICTOR: "Where do we have to go to have our picture taken?"
INSTRUCTOR: "NO! NO! NO! NO! What I meant was if you understood everything I said."
VICTOR: "Yes, sir! But why didn't you say that in the first place?"
INSTRUCTOR: "Because what I said in the first place means exactly the same thing!"

Interestingly, by repeating Victor's wh-question in the next to last line of the scenario almost verbatim, the instructor was displaying his irritation that such a simple statement in English could be so profoundly misunderstood. Often the repetition of the question in the answer is a signal of impatience or annoyance.

Tag questions comprise the third category of interrogatives. A tag question, in form, is a question word at the end of a statement which is used to express doubt, affirmation, confrontation, and/or opinion. Tag questions are useful little markers if you are interested in overpowering your opponent in an argument, heightening the conflict between you. Not long ago, I was privy to an argument between two individuals, a man and a woman who were unknown to me, outside a movie theater. I'm not sure what the two individuals were arguing about, but it became a real "knock-down, drag-out." As the pair continued to argue, the man ended every point of the case he was making with the tag, "Right?" This, in turn, so infuriated the woman that she finally stormed off, leaving the man holding two movie tickets while those who were subjected to his bullying tirades gave him disapproving stares. And what made his tirades bullying? Besides the loudness of his voice and his vociferous personality, the tag question "Right?" served to add emphasis and the heightened sense of confrontation to an escalating argument.

Tag questions are interesting not only in the ways they function, but also by the variety of tag forms used. This is especially true of negative tags used in expressions with modals. For instance, you have a friend who is suffering from an infection of some sort. Your friend has a fever and feels like "death warmed over" (see the chapter on prepositions). You are talking to friend #2 about friend #1's condition. You might say something like, "He should go to a doctor, shouldn't he?" Or, to use another example, you are a sailing instructor and you want one of your students to perform a complicated jibbing maneuver that you've gone over in class many times. You ask the student, "You can do this, can't you?" The point is, some modals like *can*, *could*, and *should* are regularly used as tags. But in the southern Appalachians as well as in many parts of the southern U.S., speakers tag with modals not commonly used as tags, such as *might* and *ought*. To friend #2 in the first scenario, a speaker may say, "He might oughta go to the doctor, mighten he?" The *mighten* could be replaced by *oughten*: "He might oughta go to the doctor, oughten he?" *Mighten* and *oughten* are abbreviated ways of saying "might not he" and "ought not he," respectively. While *mighten* and *oughten* are used frequently in certain situations and considered dialectally appropriate speech, using the full tags "might not he" and "ought not he" would be awkward, even to the point of being viewed as ungrammatical speech.

THE POWERS THAT BE

Next, this chapter will consider the third component of the manipulative triumvirate, **imperatives**, or command forms. Command forms, while usually in the form of second-person imperatives, as in "Go to your room," can also be fashioned in the first-person singular and plural, as in "Let's go to the movies this evening," or, if I am trying to end a conversation, "Let me run!" And the third person, as in the famous line uttered by Marie Antoinette, "Let them eat cake!"

Linguist Tom Givon, in his fairly recent and extensive work on English grammar, indicates that imperatives by and large are about power, the power to change the present state of the world to a more desirable one. The effectiveness of a command rests in the authority of the one who wants the change to make the change happen. Givon expresses it this way: the higher the status of the one giving the command, the greater the obligation on the part of the one being commanded. The command*er* in these cases does not need to be especially deferential or polite to the command*ee*, although he or she may decide to be polite in order to preserve any previously established decorum or relationships. Conversely, according to Givon, the higher the status of the one being commanded, the less obligation there is for him or her to comply with the command, and the greater the obligation exists on the part of the one giving the command to be deferential. Certain situations may arise, however, wherein the lower-status command*er* may become less

7. Negatives, Interrogatives and Imperatives 121

deferential to the higher-status command*ee*. The following two situations illustrate, on the one hand, respectfulness in a higher-status situation and, conversely, directness in a low-status circumstance.

As a university professor, I often find myself in the position of using imperatives. I want my students to read a chapter in the text, to complete a case study, or to make an oral presentation. A simple command form usually gets the job done. The command is not directed in a rude or overbearing way nor in a loud obstreperous voice, as in *"Read the chapter now!!!"* (imagine loud and obstreperous). But the assignment is effected using a second person imperative, a command, and I expect the students to have completed the assignment for the next class or whenever the assigned time of completion occurs. I do not need to be overly deferential, because, after all, I am the professor, and as professor, I possess a higher status in the class due to my knowledge of the subject, and due to the hierarchies within the culture of academe (although some of these hierarchies are being challenged of late by consumerist attitudes and marketplace realities). However, I am most always polite and the least bit deferential. Why? It is not so much that I want to avoid conflict, although conflict avoidance is in many cases desirable. It is not so much that I want to cede power to my students. Rather, I am respectful toward my students, and while commanding them to do something, the task is usually completed with little difficulty.

Now, suppose I were a student pilot learning to fly a Gulfstream 550, one of the most well-appointed and powerful business jets available on the market. Incidentally, my use of the subjunctive above indicates that I am in dream-speech, not that I have ever flown one. Flying a Gulfstream 550 requires a crew of two, and is most efficiently accomplished when the two are working together in harmony to ensure that the flight is safe. Suppose my instructor has asked me to land the plane while he maintains his designation of "pilot-in-command" for the training flight.

In aviation, it is important to keep in mind that flight procedures happen sequentially. In a Cessna 150, a stable and slow airplane, these procedures occur gradually until you are 50 or so feet above the ground in a landing configuration. Then the procedures occur more rapidly. By contrast, everything happens a whole lot faster in a Gulfstream. Pilots, therefore, cannot afford to be deferential to a higher-ranking colleague. "It may be good, if at this time, you could possibly lower the flaps to 40 degrees," would not work because, by the time you got the words out of your mouth, you would be hurtling toward the earth much faster than you need to be toward a landing which will cause the fillings of your teeth and the teeth of the flight crew and passengers to be strewn about the cabin.

So let's go back to our scenario, in which I am the pilot landing the Gulfstream with my instructor by my side. As I move through the checklist, I will instruct my pilot colleague to do certain things. I will maintain a professional demeanor (I will not shout out commands — even the largest flight decks are too small for shouts unless some kind of emergency befalls the flight, and even that situation calls for a firm voice only). But, to an outside observer, my instructions may seem abrupt: "Flaps 40," "Gear down," etc. During the landing, I am still second-in-command, but the context in which I find myself supersedes the need for deference.

Givon illustrates the manner by which a direct command, such as "Do your homework!" may be made more polite. Lengthening the clause by which the command is given can soften the order: "If you haven't done your homework yet, go and do it before we sit down for supper." Phrasing the command as a question also moderates the command a bit: "Have you finished your homework yet?" Using a modal, often paired with negation, creates a more polite imperative: "Shouldn't you be working on your homework?" Finally, as discovered in the previous chapter, the subjunctive often serves as a polite command: "If I were you I would do my homework before dinner."

Manipulatives and the Four Perspectives

In this discussion, the form and function of manipulative speech acts has been discovered. To conclude this chapter, this section examines how manipulatives interface with the **Four Perspectives** that form one of the foundational pillars of this handbook.

In terms of the **Perspective of Focus**, a manipulative speech act directs the discoursal focus onto the manipulator, that is, the one making a declaration, asking a question or giving a command. Simply by using a manipulative speech act, the speaker is placing a high degree of focus on his or her point of view that the established norms, however they exist, need to be in some way changed.

Immediacy is what is of greatest importance in terms of the intersection between manipulatives and the **Perspective of Time and Space**. The strength of the speech act, whether it be the use of a negative or a direct question or command in discourse, signals the hearer that the needed change in the established norm or status quo needs is of urgent importance. Likewise, deferential speech acts can be used to signal the hearer that the change in status does not need to be immediate.

Concerning the **Perspective of Condition**, the strength of the speech act often signals the degree to which the established norm will be changed. The stronger the speech act and the greater the degree of power and authority the speaker has over the hearer, the greater the potential that the established norm or the status quo will be changed.

Finally, as has been discussed in some depth, speech acts are largely about relationships (the **Perspective of Interaction**). Power and authority, negotiation and politeness are all important features of the relationship between interlocutors as they try to enable each other to understand who they are, why they want what they want, and when it is they want it.

Now You Try It!

Scripts, Speech Acts & Pragmatics

The goal of this exercise is to become familiar with functions of language, and how structures of language differ depending upon speaker intent and upon the sociocultural context in which language happens. Specifically, this will focus on scripted speech in defined situations, and will be in three phases:

- Phase One: Introduction — scripted situations
- Phase Two: Exploring — language used in scripted situations
- Phase Three: Creating — speech acts and teaching

Introduction: Consider those situations in which speakers say much the same things whenever they find themselves in the situation. For example, before getting a haircut, the barber/stylist will usually say, "How would you like it cut today?" And the customer will say something like, "just a little off the sides and top, maybe about a half an inch." This is just one of a myriad of examples. Each group should come up with at least three situations where there is little variation in language.

Exploring: What is specifically said in those situations comprises the "script" of the situation. Construct scripts from Phase One above in terms of degree of formality (formal, informal, slang). Then describe the scripts grammatically (what structures are used) and in terms of prosodics: Which words receive stress? What is the pitch contour of the script? When in your culture is it appropriate to use a slang script vs. a formal one? When should a more formal script be used? What happens if a non-native speaker puts emphasis on the wrong word in the sentence? What roles do negatives, interrogatives and imperatives play in these scripts?

Creating: What specific activities would you use to teach these speech acts?

8
Passives: Getting Yourself Invited to Izabela's Party

THE QUESTION

Not long ago, I had an international graduate student working on English with me. She was struggling with trying to get a degree in one of the sciences. In one particular summer class, which fully occupied many of her waking hours, she was required to write at least one fairly major paper every week. She would happily, although wearily, comply, but she grew increasingly frustrated with the class. The frustration arose around one relatively minor sticking point. Her grades on the papers were consistently low. She would do all the right things, write multiple drafts, get native-speaker peers to read and correct her works. But to no avail. She would get the papers back with the same general comment, "Your paper is not objective enough. You inject too much of yourself in the research." Bewildered, she came to my office with four papers she had written, all bearing the same comment, and asked me to have a look to see if I could discover what the deal was. On first read, everything looked good. In fact, she argued her point rationally and logically. I couldn't see anything which would merit the comment — that is, until I read the paper and the professor's comments a second time. And then something struck me as odd. While her data were analyzed with precision, while her argument was sound, I noticed that there were no passive sentences in the entire paper.

Scientific writing employs more passive constructions than any other form of writing. Interestingly, people do not use them as much in speaking. So when the student came back to my office, we changed many of the active sentences to passive, and, voila, the next paper was a success, all because of a marvelously simple change in grammatical voice, which caused an enormously important change in focus.

Passives and the Perspective of Focus

The passive, as are the other elements of English grammar discussed in this examination, is about perspective. While the passive encompasses the perspective of time and space, the perspective of condition, and the perspective of interaction, what passives do most effectively is reflect focus. More precisely, passives shift point of view. Being passive (in the grammatical sense and not in the sense of being unreceptive) is a way of thinking about an event from the perspective of the one who undergoes or experiences it. Passives as grammatical constructions are not greatly difficult. The object of a transitive verb (a verb which takes an object) is moved to the subject position. A "be" or "get" or "have" auxiliary is inserted. The original verb changes to the past participle, and one either deletes the original subject or puts in a by-phrase somewhere after the verb.

So what's the big deal? It is not so much that passives are hard to construct that causes problems. It is not even that passives are used in the first place that causes problems. They are used frequently, in speech, in newspapers (even though journalism teachers tell budding journalists not to use them), and in scientific textbooks. The difficulties lie in the subtle differences in meaning depending upon which of those little helping verbs one decides to use. The following story illustrates this.

The Party to End All Parties: A Personal Story

I'm one of the lucky ones, I guess you'd say. When the invitation arrived in the mail, an invitation I thought would never come, I was thrilled. For my plan worked to absolute perfection, a plan tried by many and failed by all. I am the only one who had succeeded. Here's how it happened that I got myself invited to Izabela's party.

You may or may not know that Izabela is the grand dame of the local social scene. Every year, Izabela throws *the* party of parties, and everyone who is anyone and everyone who is no one wants to go to it. In fact, the party is so wildly popular that whole in-crowds are formed around who has been to the party and who wants to be invited. The somebodies of the city, the in-crowd, are determined by who attended Izabela's party that year. And with the exception of 10 or 15 people — all Izabela's good friends, called "the chosen few" by people living in town — the list of invitees changes every year.

Some people find themselves, through no design of their own, inexplicably on the list. Others, certain that they will be included, only find empty mailboxes. The list is the best-kept secret in town. Only Izabela herself knows it. About three months before the party, held the first week in June, neighbors start asking neighbors, "Have you been invited yet? I wonder who'll be on the list this year?"

People of the city have been known to go to great lengths to try to wheedle an invitation from Izabela, including slipping her a few thousand dollars in the mail, only to have it returned as refused mail with a polite note scribbled on the back which says, "Nice Try!" Izabela has been known to be treated to lavish meals which she enjoys uncommitedly, invited to sit on boards of corporations which she accepts graciously, only to refuse to include her benefactors on her guest list.

That is until this year! I came to the city quite by accident from my native Cape Verde, San Antão to be exact. I am a dancer by trade. People say I am very handsome, can dance like Astaire, and have been known to attract my share of women. The night of the dance demonstration was no exception. The beautiful raven-haired woman in the corner caught my eye as I was about to go on stage. I decided to dance for her. Every movement, every step, every turn, every pirouette I made for her to catch her attention. And catch her attention I did. After the demonstration, we were introduced. At that moment, my heart was hooked. I knew I could not live without her. I would do anything just to be in her presence. But there was a problem. Although I am a good dancer, some even say a great dancer, I am a poor dancer in the monetary sense. She is a beautiful rich woman with plenty of friends and plenty of connections. I knew I could never realize my dream.

Eventually, I heard about Izabela's party being the social event of the year, but as a foreigner I was not familiar with the social customs of the community and the intricate rituals involved in Izabela's party. Nor did I particularly care. I just knew I wanted to be with her.

One day, quite by happenstance, I ran into Izabela downtown. I invited her to lunch which, to my surprise, she accepted. Sometime during the lunch conversation, I did the unthinkable. I asked her if I could come to her party (I did not know you couldn't ask, nor did I know no one ever did this for fear of being permanently blackballed). But, again, much to my surprise, she agreed. I did not know until later that she too had the same infatuation. Now I am on her permanent list, as Mr. Izabela. What a wonderful memory. It's been 20 years now. The party still goes on every year, and the list is as exclusive as ever. But people are still talking about how I,

Clement Dees, a poor dancer from San Antão, Cape Verde, got invited to Izabela's party.

BEING, GETTING AND HAVING

The story told from the perspective of Clement Dees is illustrative of how important focus is to narrative, spoken and written. The story is told from Clement's perspective, and as such he is the main player. And yet, the story also concerns Izabela, her party and the social structure of the town. Izabela is the only one who possesses the legitimacy to invite; she is the agent. Clement is the undergoer, to be sure, and likewise, one who takes some responsibility for Izabela's acting in the manner she acts. His actions in part facilitate his invitation. Clement **got** invited to the party. If he merely received an invitation without prompting it, he was invited to the party. And that's the rub with the passive.

There are three of them: the *be* passive, the *get* passive and the *have* passive. The three have similar forms: each uses *be*, *get*, or *have* as an auxiliary, plus the past participle of the main verb. However, they do not carry the same meaning. To illustrate this, consider the following scenarios.

Scenario 1

You are a police officer in Pembrotanck. You're off duty sitting out on your deck enjoying some peace and quiet when your next-door neighbor comes running over to your place in a panic. It seems her husband Jim went to the ATM at the bank, got out of the car, and left it running (it was a hot day). Just as Jim put his card into the machine, someone got into Jim's car and drove off with it. Seeing you relaxing on your deck, your neighbor runs up and shouts, "Can you help us? Jim's car **was** just stolen."

Scenario 2

You are a police officer in Pembrotanck. You're off duty sitting out on your deck enjoying some peace and quiet when your next-door neighbor drops over for some refreshment. In the midst of the visit, the neighbor allows that her husband, Jim, stopped by the ATM to get some money. Unfortunately, this particular ATM was in a bad part of town. Jim just happened to be passing through it on his way home from work, and needing some money for the weekend, he stopped at the ATM, knowing full well that this was not the safest neighborhood. Well, he got out of the car, leaving it running (it was a hot day). Just as Jim put his card into the machine, someone got into Jim's car and drove off with it. Your neighbor says with some exasperation, "I tell him over and over about that neighborhood. Now, Jim's gone and **gotten** his car stolen."

Scenario 3

You are a police officer in Pembrotanck. You're on duty in the precinct when your lieutenant comes over and asks you to have a look as this case file. It seems one James Cottrell, the Jim who is your neighbor, has just filed a damage claim with his insurance company for $100,000, for cost incurred for his stolen BMW, plus pain and suffering for the inconvenience. The lieutenant asks you to look into this because something just said to him that all was not copacetic. So you dig into the case and find that this was Jim's fourth insurance claim over the last four years. Same MO, same result, $100,000 in damages. Reporting back to the lieutenant, you say, "It's a clear case of fraud. Jim **had** his car stolen so he could collect the insurance. Let's book him!"

Three scenarios, ending in responses all using the passive, but with different meanings. In the first scenario, the *be* passive, the neighbor is simply reporting the theft of Jim's car. Although you could make a case for some culpability on Jim's part, blame is not the issue. What is at issue is that fact that Jim underwent an act of thievery perpetrated by some unknown agent. Jim carries the empathy (see Chapter 1). And thus it is with *be* passives. Used primarily to emphasize the undergoer of an action, *be* passives are employed when the speaker wants to be objective, not reveal a source of information, to be polite, or if the one causing the action is very well known.

In the second scenario, using a *get* passive, Jim has some overt culpability in the theft, and the speaker is acknowledging the culpability. What is being emphasized here is the thievery and Jim's actions enabling the theft. The third scenario is like the second in that Jim's car was stolen, and he bears some responsibility for the theft (he likely planned it). But unlike a *get* passive, a *have* passive appears to denote either a stronger degree of responsibility, as in the story above, or a higher degree of formality, depending upon the discourse.

And while there is no great mystery in the workings of the passive, it is important to realize the subtle differences in the *be*, *get* and *have* passives. As in the other grammatical issues discussed in these pages, the passive is a discoursal tool at the disposal of speakers and writers to co-construct and negotiate perspective.

8. Passives

Now You Try It!

Consider the following pairs of sentences from Celce-Murcia and Larsen-Freeman:

- John was hurt in the accident.
- John got hurt in the accident.
- He was invited to the party.
- He got invited to the party.
- Julie's car was stolen last weekend.
- Julie got her car stolen last weekend.
- Julie had her car stolen last weekend.
- The star can be seen from the balcony.
- The star could be seen from the balcony.
- Johnson should be elected mayor.
- Johnson should have been elected mayor.
- The red balloon was burst.
- The red balloon burst.
- We were sitting quietly by the fire when suddenly the door was opened.
- We sat by the fire when suddenly the door was opened.
- The boy spun the top.
- The top was spun by the boy.
- The top spun.

What do you see as the differences in meaning? Invent a scenario for each of these passives. How does the passive influence meaning? How does the passive in combination with the perfect and the progressive influence meaning?

9
Modals: Meeting Kelly By the Tree

THE QUESTION

Every Thursday, a group of students from my English for Internationals class and I get together to have a freewheeling conversation about any topic relating to the English language. Invariably, at least one grammar question is raised, and the question is almost always one that requires a thoughtful answer.

One particular Thursday, Melissa Carias, a bright, inquisitive MBA student from Honduras, asked the question, "What is the difference between **can** and **may**?" Immediately, I was transported back to Garden City Elementary School in Jacksonville, Florida, where I first became a grammarian, and where the difference between **can** and **may** was first explained in lurid detail to me. On one particular day in the early '60s, I can't remember which day it was, I found myself in desperate need to go to the bathroom. I was not a particularly sheepish child, so I immediately raised my hand. "**Can** I go to the bathroom?" Whereupon the teacher responded, "I don't know, **can** you?" I assured her that I sure could at the time. In fact, if I didn't start down the hall soon, I would leave a trail that would rival the best efforts of Hansel and Gretel. "It's '**May** I go to the bathroom?'" "Yes ma'am. **May** I go to the bathroom?" I barely made it. We really could have dispensed with the grammar lesson on that particular occasion.

Later, during my first iteration of graduate school, I had a professor whose field was theology, but he fancied himself a grammarian. I remember sitting at the lunch table with him one day, when I quite innocently asked, "Can you pass the salt, please?" His answer, "Yes!" No effort to pick up the shaker and send it my way, nothing, just "Yes!" You would think I would have learned the lesson from elementary school. But, alas, I was (and still am) destined to repeat these foolish grammatical faux pas. He would not pass the salt until I asked him properly, "Please pass the salt." Pride was at issue here. Everybody knows "Can you pass the salt?" means you physically pick the salt shaker up and hand it to me or slide it my way. But he wouldn't budge, and I had to eat my beets unseasoned. I could have done without the grammar lesson then too.

So what is the difference between **can** and **may**? Now that I am a full-fledged grammarian with a couple of degrees and a certificate or two behind my name to back up that claim, I can say with some assuredness that there is very little difference between **can** and **may** when used in the contexts above. I have also come to believe that answers like, "It's '**May** I go to the bathroom?,'" or "Yes!" to the request for salt and not passing it, are terribly inappropriate, and reflect more a lack of grammatical savvy than grammatical sophistication and appropriateness. I can also say with some assuredness that there is a lot of difference between **can** and **may** when used in a situation such as when a friend of yours asks, "Can you ride your bicycle 100 miles?" and you answer, "No I can't. I used to be able to." *Can*, here, denotes pure ability, not asking someone for permission. The spirit may want to but the body has other plans.

Modality

Fortunately, the basics on modals are not that difficult to figure out. Modals are verbs. But unlike most verb forms, modals do not carry tense. For example, there is no past tense of the modal **will**, since **will** commonly refers to some act that has not happened yet. One can talk about a will-kind of action as if had already been completed by attaching the perfect, but **will** itself cannot be inflected in the past. There does, however, seem to be instances where **could** denotes the past of **can**. For example, to the question "Can you ride your bike 100 miles?," rather than, "No, I can't anymore," you might reply, "I **could**, but not anymore."

Modals have a rather wide range of meaning

Modals	Phrase-Type Modals
will	be going to, be about to
must	have to, have got to, be to
should	be supposed to, ought to
would	used to
may	be allowed to
might	be able to
can	
could	

Figure 17: List of Modals. As Suggested by Celce-Murcia and Larsen-Freeman in *The Grammar Book*.

depending upon the intent of the speaker and the context of the situation. Linguists Marianne Celce-Murcia and Diane Larsen-Freeman explain many of these uses.[1]

Modals can have social uses, such as making requests, as in "Can you help me with my homework?" You can also substitute the modals **could**, **will** and **would** in this discourse.

As was the case with, "**Can** I go to the bathroom?," modals ask permission. **May**, **might**, and **could** serve this purpose as well. Interestingly, **would**, **might** and **could** are often perceived by some native speakers as being more polite requests. More will be discovered about this phenomenon later.

Another use for modals, as pointed out by Celce-Murcia and Larsen-Freeman, is logical possibility, prediction or inference. They go on to argue that certain modals carry more degree of certainty, while others less of a degree. **Could** and **might** are least certain on their scale, while **will** comprises the most certain.

Other meanings of modals include ability, as in "I can speak Spanish" and "I am able to leap over my house in a single bound"; desire, as in "I would like to go to that little romantic bistro with you this evening"; offer, as in "Would you like to sample my $18,000-a-bottle '88 Chateau d'Yquem?"; and preference, as in "I would rather study English than math."

Modals in their form and function, devoid of contextual and cultural features, offer few problems for non-native speakers. Add in those contextual and cultural features, and there are intricacies ready to leap up and grab the unsuspecting (and the unsuspecting may be a native speaker as well). Some of these intricacies not covered in the typical English grammar classroom and textbook will be covered here. For instance, how can one use modals to say "yes" and "no, not on your life"?

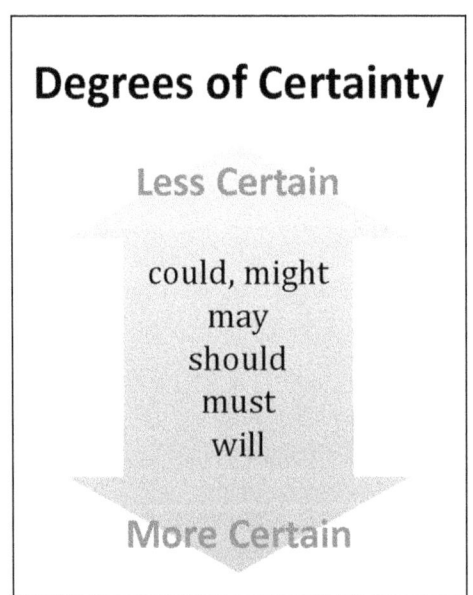

Figure 18: Modality Continuum. Representation of the degree of certainty expressed by epistemic modals.

9. Modals

How can modals be put together to be extremely polite, even when you may not want to be?

Meeting Kelly By the Tree

The following examples reveal a use of modals that I had never considered, but found very interesting when one of my native-speaker students pointed it out. How can you say "absolutely yes" or "absolutely no" with a modal? This seems on the surface to defy every traditional "rule" of the function of modality. Defy it does, but it also widens the perspective about how modals really function in the context of a particular speech community with its unique cultural values.

Scene I

Jim had been previously observed by members of the class kissing Kelly out by an expansively shady maple tree across from the cafeteria. This event itself would not have been particularly unusual except for the fact that no member of the class had ever seen Kelly publicly displaying any affection to any man nor, as a matter of fact and principle, doing anything untoward. But the students were surprised by this and came breathlessly running up five flights of stairs to my office to report the startling event.

Now, quite unknown to those breathless student onlookers, Kelly was quite taken with Jim's advance. In fact, she had had her eyes set on Jim for a while. He was in an on-campus club with her, and seemed to her to be both friendly and caring, rather different from most of the other students she had dated since her arrival on campus some four years ago. Not long after the "tree" event, Jim met Kelly in front of the cafeteria and asked her if she would like to meet him at the coffee house later that afternoon. Kelly, thrilled with the invitation but not wanting to seem too eager, told Jim, "I might if I can finish my homework." Kelly's body language betrayed her words, saying to Jim that she would make every effort to be there. Jim smiled and left, saying as he went, "I'll probably see you later, then."

Scene II

Jim had been previously observed by members of the class kissing Kelly out by an expansively shady maple tree across from the cafeteria. This event itself would not have been particularly unusual except for the fact that no member of the class had ever seen Kelly publicly displaying any affection to any man nor, as a matter of fact and principle, doing anything untoward. But the students were surprised by this and came breathlessly running up five flights of stairs to my office to report the startling event.

Now, quite unknown to those breathless student onlookers, Kelly was not the least bit impressed with this advance. In fact, part of her told her that she was actually repulsed by the whole affair. Besides, Jim, albeit friendly enough, was only a sophomore, a little young to date a senior, and he was given to childish pranks in the on-campus club they were both in. Not long after the "tree" event, Jim met Kelly in front of the cafeteria and asked her if she would like to meet him at the coffee house later that afternoon. Kelly, less than thrilled with the invitation but not wanting to seem impolite, told Jim, "I might but I have homework to do." To which Jim pleaded his case. "Come on, Kelly, all we're going to do is have some coffee and talk. Why don't you want to go?" At which Kelly ended the conversation by saying, "I said I might!" As Jim walked off, he said, "Please come, Kelly, I really want to talk to you. Besides, we'll have a good time." Kelly never showed. Jim wasn't surprised.

These *contr'actes* reveal the inherent difficulties with traditional approaches to modality, and point up the importance of context and culture, this pervasive notion of *Negotiated Perspective*, when one attempts to interpret a modal's true meaning. Simply put, in the first act, Kelly is saying "Yes!" to Jim. In the second, she is saying "No!"

You may be asking yourselves at this point, why doesn't she come right out and say yes or no? From her cultural perspective, she is doing just that. There is no need to be either more or less direct than that. But, you see, Kelly comes from a traditional Southern rural family. She was taught that politeness is very important in human interaction to maintain the stability of the community. She was also taught that "proper" girls neither seem too eager for affection nor too eager to reject a potential suitor (pardon the archaic language). And if the potential suitor is to be rejected, she was taught that the rejection must be very polite. In this speech community, "I will never meet you under a tree, in a coffee shop, or anywhere else for that matter, at any time now or forever, bucko," would be inappropriate in every case. In Scene I, both Jim and Kelly are willing participants. Both want to meet at the coffee house.

We'll See!

When I was a rambunctious kid, I used to conceive of all manner of activities my dad could do with me. It usually involved something to do with aviation. "Hey, Dad, let's go over to the airport and watch the planes come in." "Hey, Dad, could you arrange for us to fly on a Martin 404 [one of those famous, reliable old propliners of the 1950s and 1960s]?" Of course, some of the requests were met with enthusiasm. Some were met with less enthusiasm, especially when it meant having to spend large sums of money, which we did not have. But rather than quelling my youthful enthusiasm, where everything was possible and inexpensive, my father would simply say, "We'll see." Now, the expression "we'll see" may, in certain circumstances, mean "yes," or, at least, there is a fairly high probability that the request will be met. But many times, "we'll see" means "no." Rather than directly saying, "no," "we'll see" conveys the same message while retaining the appropriate degree of politeness required by the culture of the speech community. What is interesting is that those from the speech community where this form of "we'll see" is prevalent, which includes a very large part of the southern United States, and, I suspect, parts of the Middle Atlantic around the middle Appalachians, do not follow up a later time whether the "we'll see" has turned into a yes or no. It is understood that "we'll see" means "no." There is no reason to follow up.

THE WHYS OF DOUBLE AND TRIPLE MODALS

One of the most interesting uses of modals in these parts and in most of the South is that speakers tend to pile them up, one on top of the other. I have been asked countless times by folks who are not of the Southern persuasion why we do this. The fact is most dialects have double modals but may not be aware of it. But in the South, we have perfected the art of double modal use.

Here are just a few double modals used frequently in Southern dialect: might ought to, used to could, may ought to, might could, might can, might should, may should, might have to, may have to, might be allowed to, may be allowed to, may be going to, might be going to, should ought to, should have to, should be allowed to, and the list goes on. So why do we use this unique construction? The simple answer is that it has cultural roots. Sometimes, but not always, we here in the South use a more indirect form of communication. In other words, we may talk round about a subject before we actually hit it dead on.

As the film on American speech, *American Tongues*, so nicely points out, if a Southerner from the Appalachian region, for example, wants to conduct business with someone, the Southerner might talk a while, either touching base with someone he knows or getting to know someone he does not. It is conceivable for the conversation to take as much as 30 minutes to complete before business begins. Incidentally, it is changing somewhat as the pace of life quickens.[2]

Paired with indirectness is the idea that almost every Southerner learns, an idea that has been passed down from generation to generation: that it is important to be polite. The old adage, "If you can't say something nice about someone, don't say anything at all," still holds in many parts of the South.

The use of double modals is the grammatical means to be both indirect and polite. If one wanted to tell someone else what to do, or if one wanted to give someone else some friendly advice that he likely would not want to immediately heed, one might say something like, "You might want to clean your room, company is coming." That is far more polite than, "Clean this room up now!" (even though there is a place for very direct commands that are not necessarily polite). Likewise, if one was asked to do something that one really do not want to do, it is not polite to turn someone down directly. The more indirect and polite way to say no is to follow the invitation with, "I might could if I get my work done." Southerners generally know that this response is a nice way of declining the invitation while at the same time leaving open the possibility that one will show up. The story of Kelly and the tree illustrates this well, as well as illustrating how one can say yes and no with modals.

Gender and Modals

The use and frequency of modals may indeed have some relationship to gender. One of my former students, Kelly Hawkins (no relation to the Kelly by the tree), completed an interesting study which correlates modal choice and frequency to gender. She studied a sizeable population of speakers of Appalachian English in and around the speech communities of Asheville and Boone, North Carolina, and compared them to speakers of varied dialects of English at Appalachian State University. Her study looked at modals of potential/certainty (see Figure 12 above) to see if men viewed the certainty continuum differently from women. What she found is interesting. She concluded that men and women do in fact view the certainty continuum differently.

The data from this population indicate that men in the Appalachian region and on the campus of Appalachian State University tend to use modals that are more direct, while women from the same sample tend to use indirect modals when asked by a friend if they would like to hang out that night. When categorizing modals according to probability, men seemed to agree more as a whole in their responses than women did. From which modals convey the most probability to the modals that convey the least probability, men listed them as follows: must/will, will, should, would, should/can, might, and may. Women, on the other hand, had a little more disagreement in the responses. From most probable to least probable, women listed the modals as follows: will, can, might, could, could/would, should, should/may/can, must/may/might, and must/may/might. In *The Grammar Book: An ESL/EFL Teacher's Course*, Celce-Murcia and Larsen-Freeman claim that **will** has the highest probability followed by **should** then **may** and then **could/might**. They do not list *must, would* or *can* (see Figure 12 above).

What we have discovered is that modals function in a variety of ways depending upon the intention of the speakers, the culture in which the speaker and hearer find themselves, and what is being communicated.

Now You Try It!

1. List of Modals

Think of scenarios where these modals may mean something different from the traditional uses of modals suggested by Celce-Murcia and Larsen-Freeman.

Modals	Phrase-Type Modals
will	be going to, be about to
must	have to, have got to
should	be supposed to, ought to
would	used to
may	be allowed to
might	
can	be able to
could	

2. Situations Abound

Write a short paragraph indicating what you might do in these situations. Use as many modals as possible.

- You are driving on a deserted mountain road, and your car develops a flat. You discover that there is no spare tire. What do you do?

- Your boyfriend said he could not go out with you tonight because he has to work, but you've just seen him with another woman coming out of the movies. What do you do?
- You have been offered a high-paying job in a local company. You badly need the money but you find the company is dishonest. What do you do?
- You notice one of your classmates cheating on the final exam. Although a lot of students cheat, you and your friend have always been against cheating. What do you do?

10
Temporal Expressions: Come By, Say, the First of the Month

THE QUESTION

Back at the English table, a very shy student from Japan, who regularly attends the weekly meetings of the table, takes copious notes, but says little, sits down and immediately asks the following question: "When is next week?" At first, I thought there was a punch line coming so I waited for a few seconds for what I was sure was to follow. But, much to my chagrin, nothing followed. It was a real question, not bait for a joke. So then, putting on my best linguist face, in my best linguist voice, I said,

"Huh?'
"When is next week?" she repeated.
"It's next week, probably starting next Monday," I replied, still rather bumfuzzled by the question.
"No, that's not what I mean. When does this week end and next week start?" she asked.
Oh, I get it, I thought to myself. The question is about the age-old problem of telling time, a problem rooted in our very perspectives of culture.
"Well, it depends. I don't mean my answer to be vague, nor do I mean that your question is not important. In fact, it is very important. But it does depend on where you are, who you are with and when you are there." A good beginning, don't you think?
"Huh?" the student replied.
"Think of it this way. Right now it is Tuesday, almost the middle of the week, but not quite. If I ask you what will you do *this* weekend, I am referring to the weekend beginning three days from now, *this* Friday. Likewise, if I ask you what *did* you do *last* weekend, I am referring to the weekend that ended two days ago, *last* Sunday."

"Hmm!" the student responded. I thought she was beginning to see it.

"Next week, then, would start the Monday after the weekend beginning three days from now, *this* weekend."

"Hmm!" The student responded, looking even more puzzled.

So I drew it!

TIME LIKE AN EVER-ROLLING STREAM

Adverbials in general do not pose great problems for non-native English speakers. Students learning English can usually construct adverbial phrases accurately and put them in the correct place. But there is no one area under the general heading of "adverbials" which confounds non-native speakers any more than temporality expressions, specifically, in terms of their degree of specificity.

I never considered time to be of any particular difficulty until I started teaching English as a second language. Then I realized how difficult it is, especially since time reflects cultural perspectives. Some cultures fill time with activities. In these cultures one can waste it, kill it, save it. One can be on it, about it, in it, over it, through it. What is more, some cultures do one thing at a time, while still others are able to balance many activities at the same time.

The extent of the problem was revealed to me quite by accident. I happened to be talking to an administrator friend of mine about one of our international students we both admired. Amid the conversation, he let it be known that he found international students have a difficult time with

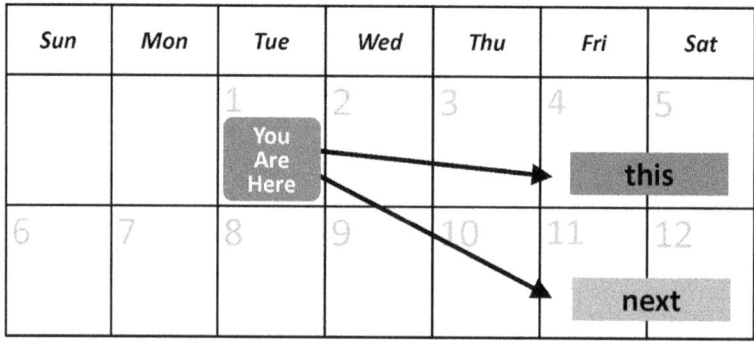

Figure 19: This Week and Next Week. Illustrating one of the more thornier problems in English grammar. The specific referent of *this* and *next* depends upon the time of speech, with Wednesday seemingly being the boundary.

appointments, especially those which are made non-specifically; appointments like, "Come by the office toward the end of next week and we'll sort things out." When is "toward the end of next week?" When is "the first of the month," "the end of the month," "the first of next week?" What is interesting is that native speakers cannot agree on the answers to these questions either.

TGIF

Returning to the original question "When is next week?," the down and dirty answer which is also the most elegant answer is, "It depends." It depends on who you are talking to, where you are talking to them, and when you are talking to them. If it's Tuesday, July 1, and someone asks you what are you going to do next weekend, and you are in Leeds, England, chances are he is referring to the weekend that starts Friday, July 4, and ends sometime on July 6 (or 7, depending upon what kind of weekend you had). But if you are in Charlotte, North Carolina, if someone asked you the same question, you may think about your activities planned for July 11–13. *This* weekend would be the 4th through the 6th, *this* referring to any time after Sunday but before Friday. *Next* happens after Friday starts.

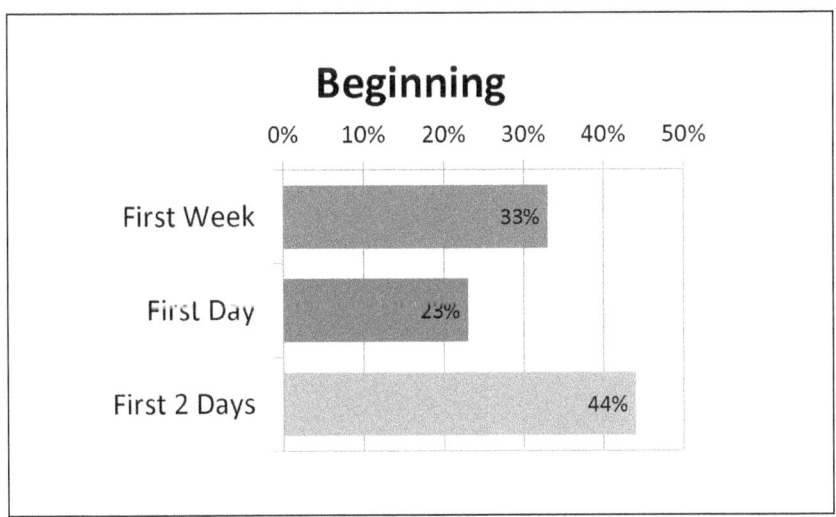

Above and following two pages and top of page 136: **Figure 20: Temporal Adverbs.** This illustration is based on a study conducted by Austin Cooke. It illustrates that time reference is often in the mind of the beholder.

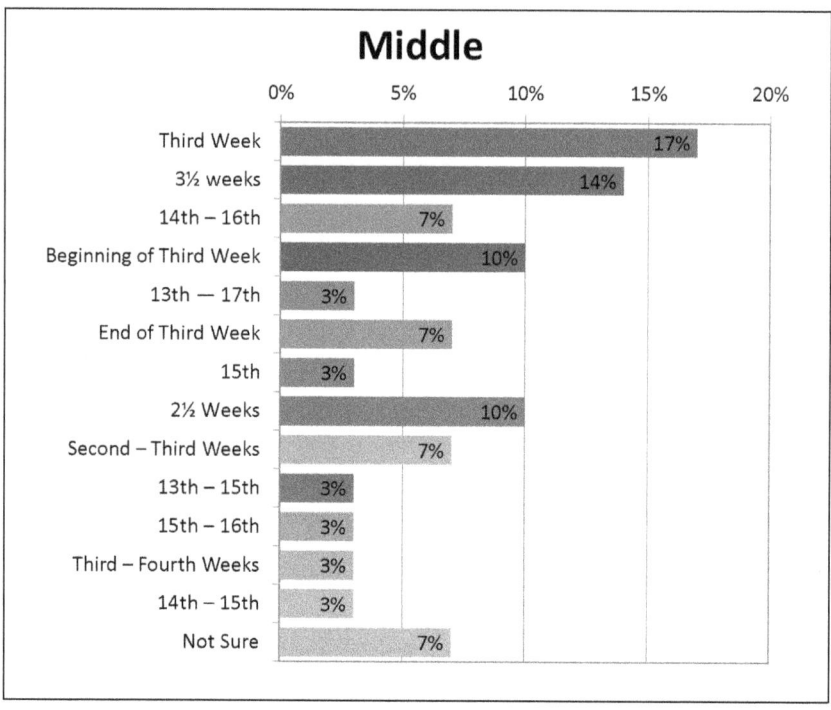

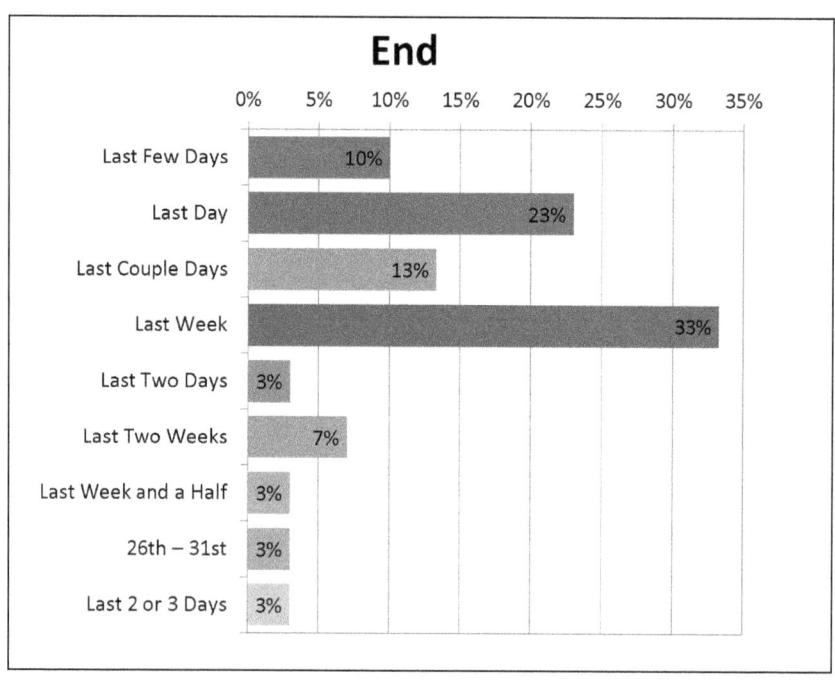

10. Temporal Expressions 143

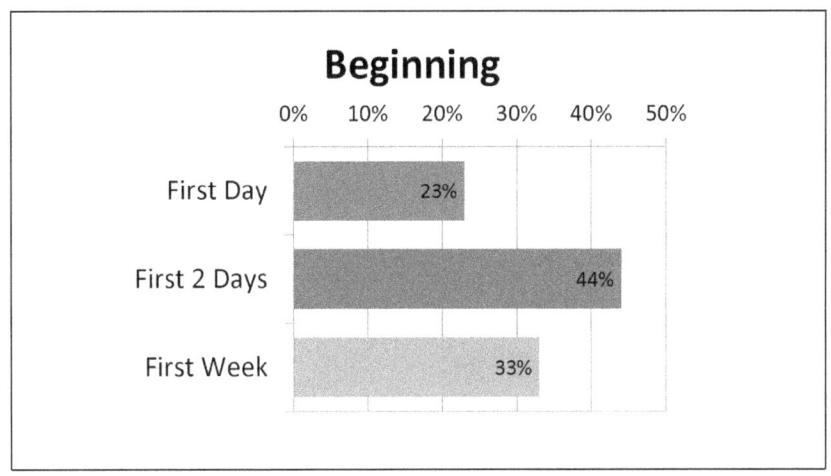

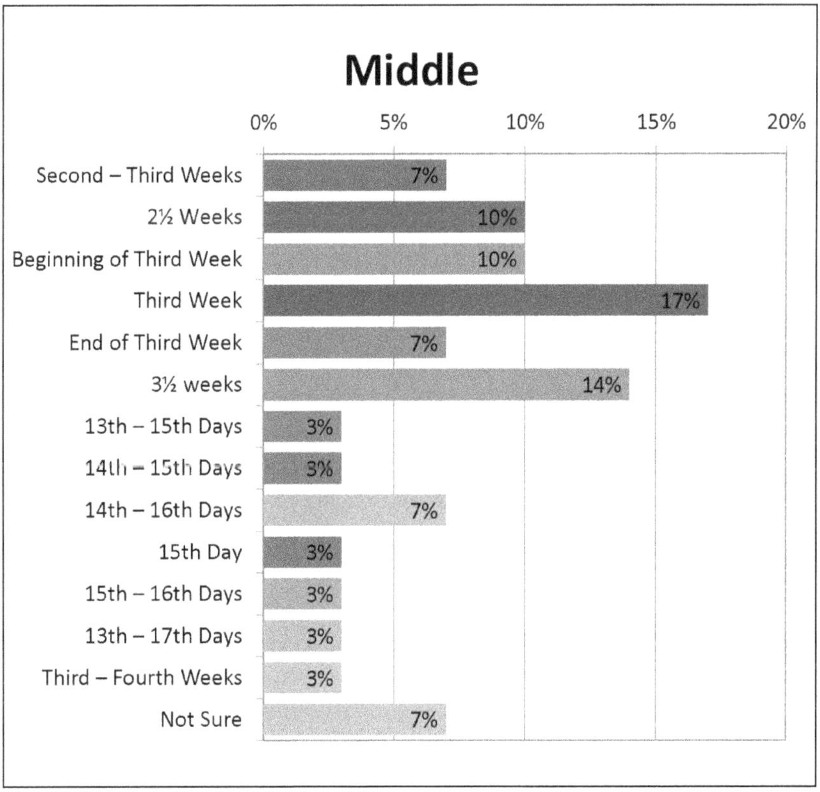

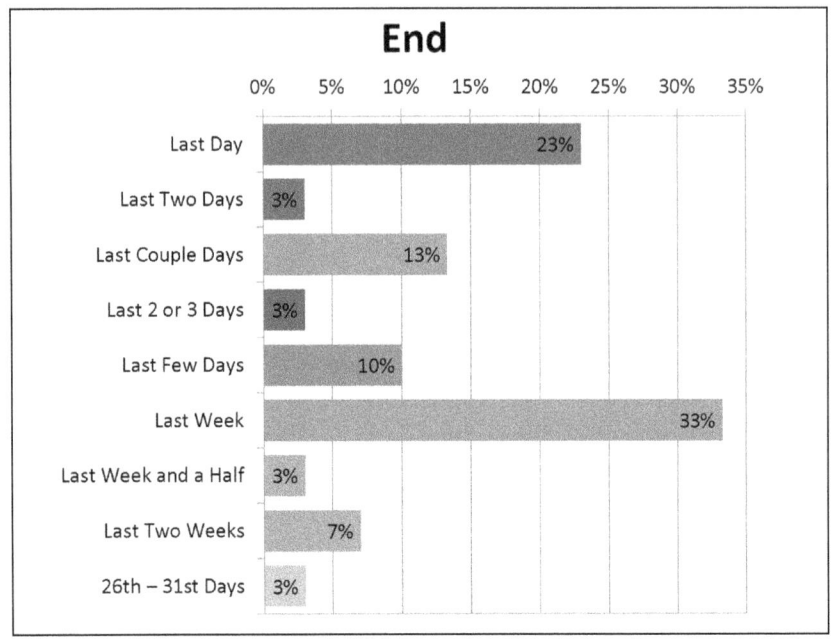

SCALES OF TIME

Non-specific time referents tend to be scalar notions dependent upon the speech community. While native speakers cannot always agree on specifics, they seem to know the parameters, although there is a bit of variation. How are these learned? Culturally, and in context. A former student of mine, Austin Cooke, completed a short study where he analyzed responses to three similar situations. The research survey asked 30 participants to respond to the following situation: One of your professors or managers (for non-students) has asked you to come by the office at the beginning/middle/end of the month for a meeting about a project. When do you arrive for the appointment? The respondents were randomly given a time for the meeting, either the beginning, middle or end of the month. The results confirmed the theory that while native-speakers possess an understanding of the limits of non-specific time, there is by no means complete agreement, and in some cases there is a wide variation in viewpoints. The graphs at the end of the chapter illustrate this.

Most of the participants in Cooke's survey indicated that most, but not a majority, believe that the "beginning of the month" is the first two days. However, a sizable percentage indicate that the "beginning of the month" is the first week. A good number deem the beginning to be the first day.

Notice there is even wider disagreement over when the "middle of the month" occurs. While many of the respondents designated the third week as the "middle of the month," almost as many said that the middle of the month is three and a half weeks into the month. But notice there were 13 different opinions about when the "middle of the month" falls.

Finally, what was discovered about the "middle of the month" holds true for the "end of the month." While many participants agreed that the "end of the month" is the last week, many others indicated that "the end of the month" is the last day. Here, too, there was a wide variance of responses.

So what does this study teach about these non-specific temporal expressions? It suggests that three factors give rise to the wide variation in understanding of non-specific time. The first factor relates to degree of specificity. In other words, these temporal expressions pose problems because what is at issue is knowing how specific someone is being. As Cooke's study demonstrated, some have a more exact definition of non-specific time while others view time more approximately. Cues lie in the context of the speech community itself. This, of course, is very difficult to generalize, but time spent in the community serves as the best teacher.

The second factor has to do with vested interest. Non-specific temporal expressions are commonly used when speakers have little vested interest in the outcome of the event. The request to "come by the office at the beginning of the month" denotes that the interaction which will take place at the office likely carries a lower level of importance for the speaker than for the listener. Reflect back to the discussion about articles in Chapter 2, where importance and specificity were linked, and it was argued that the more specific something is the more important it tends to be. Well, non-specific temporal references versus specific references to time behave in the same way. The less specific a time reference is, the less important the event surrounding the time reference is to the person who spoke it (although it may be more important to the hearer). Likewise, the more specific a time reference is, the greater degree of importance to the speaker.

For example, let's say you or one of your students or colleagues requests something of you that you know would take a great deal of time, and for which there is little reward; say you are being asked to be on a committee to plan a conference that may or may not happen because of budget constraints. You have plenty to do, and frankly, the conference is on a topic which is of little interest to you. But you have great organizational skills, and you are being asked to help plan the conference as a non-paid volunteer. The friend who asks you appeals to your good nature. Now, when asked when you could get together for a committee meeting, you may say that you have no interest in being on the committee and politely decline. But say you are not in the position to decline (see below). You may instead say that you are free sometime at the end of next month: "Get back to me later." Although you are indeed stalling, your stalling tactic may enable you to rearrange your schedule to meet the task, even though you feel you have no vested interested in the committee nor in the conference.

A third factor that influences the use of non-specific temporal expressions suggests that what may be behind their use is the power relationship between the interlocutors. In other words, vested interest may include a power component. The more power one has and the less vested interest one has, the more likely one might be to use non-specific time references. The more power one has and the more vested interest one has, the more likely one will use a specific reference. That being said, however, the level of vested interest seems to be the primary factor determining whether or not a non-specific time reference is used.

Now You Try It!

1. Replicating the Study

Using the following scenarios, conduct a survey, compile data and draw any conclusions you can about the use of non-specific temporal expressions.

- You request a meeting with your professor (or manager) to discuss a future project idea. Your professor (manager) asks you to come by the office at the beginning of next month. When do you arrive at the office?
- You request a meeting with your professor (or manager) to discuss a future project idea. Your professor (manager) asks you to come by the office the middle of next month. When do you arrive at the office?
- You request a meeting with your professor (or manager) to discuss a future project idea. Your professor (manager) asks you to come by the office at the end of next month. When do you arrive at the office?

2. When Does Next Week Begin?

Go online and search studies which tackle the confusing issue of time reference as it relates to the question, "When does this week end and next week begin?"

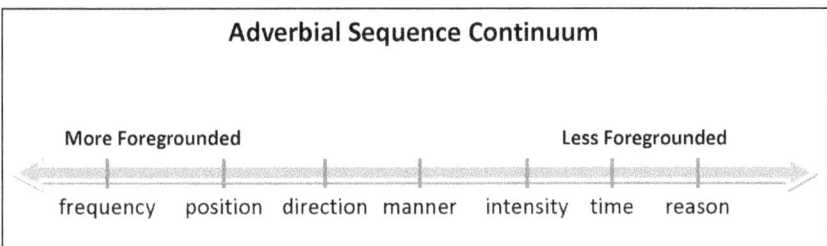

Figure 21: Adverbial Sequence Continuum. Multiple adverbs can be used in an English sentence. This continuum is based upon a study conducted in the mid-1990s by Henno Parks.

3. Other Adverbials

Hypothesis: The more concrete the adverbial the more foregrounded and closer to the beginning of the sentence it will be. The more abstract the adverbial the more backgrounded and further from the beginning of the sentence it will be unless it serves as a sentential modifier. In this case, the adverbial phrase is foregrounded.

11
Reciprocals: Backscratching

THE QUESTION

It had been a long Thursday, a cold and boring one at that. My classes moved along toward five o'clock like molasses. Winter in the mountains had stretched into what most of the rest of the South was enjoying as spring. I was tired of it, the students were tired of it. Day's end or May, for that matter, couldn't get here soon enough.

> "Any questions?" I asked as a wrap-up, with the full confidence that the students were ready to bust out of the classroom and head over to the nearest taproom to relieve the winter doldrums.
> "Yes," one of my French students said, raising his hand. "When do you use *each other* and when do you use *one another*?"
> "Hmm," I said, grasping for a quick answer, "Well, I've never thought about that one.... Well.... let's see."
> The truth is, I had thought about it, way back in graduate school, as a term project. Fortunately, I remembered the occasion.

THE ZEN OF RECIPROCALS

> "At least three times a week, Paula and Suzie help each other with their homework." The construction *each other* signals the use of a unique lexical form in English known as the reciprocal. Structurally, the reciprocal is formed from two underlying sentences in which the subject of one sentence is the subject of the other and vice versa. In the example above, Paula helps Suzie, and likewise, Suzie helps Paula. To avoid useless repetition, a reciprocal pronoun is used.
> Many languages express reciprocal action through the reciprocal pro-

noun. The Spanish example below, cited by *The Grammar Book*, is a good case in point[1]:

> Los actores *se* maquillaron antes de salir al escenario.

There are two ways to interpret this sentence.

The first image is this. Suppose one was backstage at the Theatre de Lys in Greenwich Village just before the premiere of the 1956 version of Berthold Brecht's *The Threepenny Opera*. One would see Lotte Lenya putting makeup on Edward Asner, and Bea Arthur applying foundation to the mug of Jerry Orbach. "The actors made each other up before going on stage."

In the second view, one might see a pensive Lotte Leyna going through her pre-show routine of putting on her makeup. "Now Jenny Diver..." "The actors made themselves up before going on stage."

Other languages, such as the Bantu family of languages from Eastern and Southern Africa, form the reciprocal by affixing a particle to the verb stem, as in:

> Mwalimu na wanaamkiana
> mwalimu na   wanafunzi   wa————na———amki——an———a
> noun   and noun   subj tense   stem   recip.   final vowel
> m/wa   m/wa   3 pl. pres. ind   "greet"
> "The teacher and the students greeted each other."

In this example, the infix -an- is added to the verb stem "amkia" to designate reciprocal action.

Still other languages utilize a separate verb category which indicates both the reflexive and reciprocal. For example, in Hebrew, the hithpael verbal category carries both meanings:

> Lehitkable.
> "They accepted each other."
> "They accepted themselves."

English has two forms of the reciprocal pronoun, *each other* and *one another*. These forms create few inherent problems for native and non-native speakers (and until my student asked me about it, I had never encountered a problem with it). Nevertheless, the reciprocal pronouns have traditionally been viewed as distinct and rule-governed. According to Celce-Murcia, "The usual rule given to explain is that 'each other' is used when there are two noun phrases involved whereas 'one another' is the appropriate form to use when there are more than two noun phrases."[2]

Back in graduate school, I had to choose a grammar topic on which to do research for a course in English grammar. I chose this topic; why, I haven't the faintest idea. But the study I conducted did prove somewhat interesting, even if the topic is somewhat obscure. In the next few sections is a description of the research.

METHODOLOGY

The goal of that brief study was to test the prescriptive rule. Do native speakers of English use these forms interchangeably, or do they adhere strictly to the rule? Are there any general tendencies besides the stated rule governing the use of *each other* vs. *one another* and vice versa? If so, what are these tendencies?

To test the validity of the rule, a personal preference survey was devised, consisting of five pairs of sentences, identical except for the reciprocal pronoun. The sentence pairs are as follows:

a. Sandy and Gail promised each other they would get together again.
   Sandy and Gail promised one another they would get together again.
b. After the tornado, the families of the victims helped each other.
   After the tornado, the families of the victims helped one another.
c. The bride and groom promised to love each other for the rest of their lives.
   The bride and groom promised to love one another for the rest of their lives.
d. Everyone in the club seemed to get along well with each other.
   Everyone in the club seemed to get along well with one another.
e. Ken and Doug hate each other.
   Ken and Doug hate one another.

Since the stated objective was to test reciprocal usage in common-usage English, the survey was read to the respondents. The respondents were then asked which sentence they preferred and why they chose one form of the reciprocal over the other. Surveys were taken in five different states in the United States: Wisconsin, Tennessee, South Carolina, North Carolina, and Florida. Of the respondents surveyed, 94 percent were white and 6 percent African American. There were 71 percent between the ages of 18 and 24, 23 percent between the ages of 25 and 39, and 6 percent between the ages of 40 and 80. The respondents included college students, young professionals, and blue-collar workers.

Results

The stated rule for reciprocal usage would predict that *each other* would be the preferred choice sentences a, c, and e. *One another* should be preferred in b and d.

The results of the survey indicate that, although response patterns do correspond with the predicted rule in some cases, in general, reciprocal usage does not appear to be driven by the knowledge and application of grammatical rules. Rather, the data suggest that three broad semantic/pragmatic variables appear to influence the choice of one reciprocal over the other.

First, when the respondents perceived the context of the sentence as being less formal and more casual, the overwhelming preference was *each other* even if *one another* was warranted by rule.

(1) Sandy and Gail promised each other they would get together again. 75%
Sandy and Gail promised one another they would get together again. 22%
No preference. 3%

(2) Ken and Doug hate each other. 87%
Ken and Doug hate one another. 13%

(3) After the tornado, the families of the victims helped each other. 69%
After the tornado, the families of the victims helped one another. 26%
No preference. 5%

In (1) and (2) respectively, the two noun-phrase subjects would, by rule, predict *each another*. And by a wide margin, *each other* was preferred. However, when asked about why they chose *each other*, the folks who took the survey indicated that the sentence sounded less formal, less stilted. They said that Sandy and Gail were friends, and that *each other* is what they would use when talking about friends. In (3), the perceived degree of familiarity influenced the choice of *each other* over *one another*. Several respondents indicated that they would use *each other* because it sounded as if the tornado brought the "families of the victims" close together. There was a sense of mutual need as a result of a tragic situation.

The second semantic/pragmatic factor is the converse of the first. When the respondents perceived the context of the sentence as being more formal, more idealistic or more stylized, *one another* was preferred, even if *each other* was warranted by rule.

(4) The bride and groom promised to love one another for the rest
of their lives. 52%
The bride and groom promised to love each other for the rest of
their lives. 45%
No preference. 3%

In (4), *one another* was only slightly preferred over *each other*. However, when the statement was formed into the question, "Do you promise to love (*each other, one another*) for the rest of your lives?," 98 percent preferred *one another*. Many of the respondents commented that they preferred *one another* because it sounded like very formal, ceremonial language, as if the question was being asked at a wedding service, which the respondents viewed as a formal setting.

The third issue ties in syntax with semantics and pragmatic variables. When an indefinite pronoun such as "everyone" is the subject of a reciprocal sentence, the preference chosen by a majority of respondents was *one another* over *each other*.

(5) Everyone in the club seemed to get along well with each other.   46%
Everyone in the club seemed to get along well with one another.   54%

What appears to be going on here is the notion of what I call "singularity," that is, considering a group as a single entity. Many of the respondents linked *one* another with the indefinite pronoun every*one,* which requires a singular verb. *One another*, according to many respondents, "sounds singular," thus being semantically appropriate for this sentence. It appears from the data in (5), *everyone* and *one another* have a close semantic and grammatical relationship. Changing every*one* to every*body* had no effect on the results. A majority preferred *one another* vs. *each other*.

Tendencies

What this short study showed was (and still is) that, when speakers use reciprocals in conversational English, they appear to make their decisions on which one to use on three tendencies. The first of these tendencies is that English speakers are largely unaware that there is such a thing as a rule that governs the use of reciprocals. They use them based on more pragmatic reasons such as how formal or informal the conversation seemed to them. *Each other* was strongly preferred in more casual, less formal discourse. *One another* was preferred in more formal contexts. One respondent indicated that *each other* sounded as if it should be used in spoken English and *one another* in written English. On a related note, one said in her comments that she preferred to use *each other* in every instance. So what these data seem to point out is that in actual usage, the prescriptive rule governing reciprocals is not operative.

Second, believe it or not, there were a few respondents who were actually aware of the rule, and their selections were based upon this knowledge.

When asked to comment on their choices, they simply stated the rule. However, when asked if the other choice seemed to them to be incorrect or to sound funny, they indicated that they sometimes use the other form in informal conversation, and both forms sounded correct.

Third, certain sociocultural factors, however undefined, seemed to have an effect on the outcome of at least one set of data. In the South Carolina survey, taken at a large textile manufacturing plant in the Sandhills region, the responses of those who indicated that they were "blue-collar employees" followed a particular pattern which was different from those indicating that they were young professional employees. With the exception of *each other* being preferred by 86 percent of the blue-collar respondents in, "After the tornado, the families of the victims helped each other," blue-collar employees chose *one another* in every other pair of statements by wide margins. It is difficult to pinpoint the root causes of this tendency, although one suspicion is that the choice is related in some way to perception, whether the context of the situation was more formal or less formal. Perhaps it is simply a matter of preference, or "that's what we use" in the context of their community. Maybe one day, an enthusiastic grammar student will produce a study to look into what pragmatic variables are at work here.

Conclusion

So, why do speakers of English choose one reciprocal pronoun over the other? The short answer is context. Although reciprocal usage in English does not appear to be a difficult one for ESL/EFL learners, these data point to a larger issue in language teaching. The importance of context, and one's understanding of events in context, are important motivators of grammatical choice. In communication, native speakers of English utilize a range of semantic and pragmatic variables which influence grammatical choice. One task as teachers is to enable students to engage the language in context in order that they may better understand the complexities of how English speakers communicate, how English speakers negotiate perspective.

Now You Try It!

The Study

Qualitative research studies, like the one above, enable you as a teacher to collect a variety of interesting data. Surveys, ethnographies and interviews are just some of the valuable tools you as a teacher can use to conduct research which will enhance your teaching. As a trial run at qualitative research, your task is to reduplicate the study above, using the same methodology (questionnaire). Did you get the same results? How are your results different? What other grammar issues might you use surveys and interviews to enhance your teaching?

Conclusion: The Zen of Grammar

THE ANSWER

The ideas behind the creation of this handbook were prompted by questions posed by non-native speakers of English regarding the nature of English grammar. These questions reflect the desire to not only understand how native speakers apply English in everyday settings, but also the desire to understand the speakers themselves, their ways of life, their varied behaviors, their experiences. Given both the linguistic and existential nature of this study, what can we conclude about the grammar of English? Four major themes have emerged from this book.

First theme: the grammar of English is immeasurably more than a series of binary rules applied universally. Rather, grammar comprises the framework, the scaffold by which frequently divergent individual perspectives are negotiated.

Second theme: the grammar of English is encompassed by four interconnected perspectives: the Perspective of Time and Space, the Perspective of Condition, the Perspective of Focus and the Perspective of Interaction.

Third theme: the grammar of English is a neuro-psychological discoursal phenomenon. It is difficult if not impossible to analyze grammatical form apart from the various contexts in which it functions.

Fourth theme: the grammar of English is an extremely difficult concept to comprehend separated from the speakers who employ it in spoken and written discourse. To truly understand why certain grammatical forms function in particular and often unique ways requires a journey into the minds of native speakers. Arguably, the most promising way to learn the grammar of English is by taking context into account. Put simply, much of grammar is existential.

The Existential Nature of Grammar

Before concluding this text, allow me to consider the various hats and shoes I wear. I am often seen attired in the hat of an anthropologist and neurolinguist. I sometimes wear the cap of a teacher-trainer, a teacher, and, certainly, I always wear the hat of a person, a unique individual with the perspective of fifty-some-odd years of life experience. Sometimes I wear all these hats at once, sometimes just one at a time. But my perspective on the grammar of English comes less from wearing hats than from being togged up in ill-fitting shoes: the shoes of those courageous students who decide to take the bold step to experience life as international students at my university or who decide to take the arduous journey from Central America to better their lives working in the United States. Fortunately for me, these brave persons find themselves in my English and linguistics classes asking the question "why?" I say these shoes are ill-fitting because it is difficult for me to imagine the hardships many of these students face just to walk through the door of the classroom and be trained by second-language teachers (and to train second-language teachers at the same time). But it is in the shoes of my students that I have learned the most about English grammar.

I think of a young man named Pedro Martinez (not his real name) who came to Boone, North Carolina, from Chiapas, Mexico, to work on a Christmas tree farm. Pedro was (or is) an auto mechanic, one of the best in Tuxtla. He could disassemble a Mercedes transmission or a Volkswagen Beetle engine with the deftness of a surgeon, no doubt with his eyes shut. And until political problems arose in Chiapas, he had plenty of work repairing the cars of the rich and the expanding middle class. But the growing discord between the haves and the have-nots led to violence, which eventually led to unemployment, which led to severe economic hardship. And Pedro found it difficult to support his young wife and three children. About a year earlier, Pedro's cousin, Ramon, left Chiapas in the same way Pedro was about to, and after a trying journey, found himself in the mountains of North Carolina, working as a landscaper for a nursery in Avery County. Ramon had arranged contacts for Pedro as soon as he crossed the border into the United States. Pedro would be one of the lucky ones securing a temporary work permit in the United States. He would be able to cross the heavily guarded border legally.

One Friday in March, he and his family set out in their 1980 Nissan Sunny for the 1500-mile trip from Tuxtla Gutierrez, Chiapas, to the United States border at Matamoras. The journey took almost a week, traveling from town to town, staying in cheap rooming houses, and sometimes sleeping in the car. They crossed the border and arrived in Brownsville, Texas, where they were put on a bus for Hickory, North Carolina. This journey was no less long and tiring, through states whose names held a vague acquaintance for Pedro (e.g., Texas, Oklahoma), and through states he had never heard of (e.g., Arkansas and Tennessee). As he rolled mile after countless mile through the freshly plowed rolling farmland of the South, he remembered his home in Chiapas, the lush mountains, the energy of close family, the recent turmoil. He was happy to be free of struggle, but afraid — afraid of new struggles, work, language, a new and strange culture which he had only seen in movies and occasionally on TV.

When he arrived in the mountains, he felt strangely at home. The topography was similar to Chiapas. The people seemed friendly enough. Ramon had secured housing for Pedro and his family. A week after arrival, Pedro started his job on a landscaping crew in a resort outside of Newland. The pay wasn't bad by their former standards. And there were lots of new things, so many new things that it was almost overwhelming. Surely this was a land of plenty, stores full of food and clothes and life's necessities, Walmart, Kmart, Jiffy Mart, Big Macs, Big Hardees, Big Bacon Deluxes, new and improved this and new and improved that.

Although things were going pretty well at work and at home, there was always this feeling of unease, as if they were strangers in a strange land. There were problems with the currency, and those strange stares in the aisles of the Winn-Dixie, and those accents! That they were indeed strangers in a strange land hit them like a torrent one evening in early June of their first year in the area. They decided to celebrate their eldest son Carlos's birthday at one of the local restaurants. Carlos was ecstatic about celebrating his first birthday in the U.S. Pedro and Juana Maria had taken him to a restaurant in town, a somewhat upscale cafe (that was not overly elegant but nice). When they arrived, the host looked at them strangely and seated them at the table near the kitchen. After the server had come to the table the fourth time to take their order (the were having trouble with the menu), the server said in a fairly loud and brusque voice, "Don't you understand the menu? What's the matter, can't you speak English?" They left humiliated and hurt.

Sadly, the situation with the Martinez family is not altogether unusual, especially with the increasing numbers of non-native speakers of English relocating to communities throughout the United States. When I arrived at Appalachian State University so many years ago, I was amazed by both the reality of the international community in the small town where Appalachian is located, and the potential for its growth. I had been away for a few years, in graduate school and overseas. When I lived here in the early '80s, the community was fairly homogeneous; the only international persons I would see regularly were the two or three families of Vietnamese refugees who had moved into the area under the sponsorship of local churches. When I returned, I was amazed with the increase in the number of internationals in the area, especially Spanish-speaking persons who were working in the Christmas tree industry. It was heartening to see darker complexions than mine and to hear Spanish spoken in the Winn-Dixie or at the Shady Lawn restaurant in Newland, the small county seat near Boone.

So what do the collective experiences of internationals like the Martinez family and the international students who grace my classroom have to do with grammar? On the surface, nothing, and yet, everything! Even before the first word was processed on the first page of this text, I had envisioned writing a grammar text which attempts to satisfactorily answer the question "why?" After all, "why" has certainly become one of the more prevalent questions that students pose to me in my life as a linguist. Now, even as the last words of the text are being penned, I have discovered that the true significance of the question "why?" lies in the realization that while grammatical issues in and of themselves may prompt a certain, albeit low, percentage of "why" queries (some students are genuinely curious about the inner workings of grammar), I am convinced now that the lion's share of "why" questions have little to do with grammar, or with linguistics for that matter. These questions are, at their very heart, existential ones. When a student asks, "What is the difference between can and may?" or "When do you use less, and when do you use fewer?," what he really wants to know is, "How is it you use your language (in this case, English) so that you can fit into this particular speech community?" Stated more precisely, the question of "why" seems more an entreaty than a question: "Please help me assimilate into this culture by teaching me how to speak (and write) appropriately."

If such be the case, and I firmly believe that it is, then the focus of this text is right on target: the answer to "why" has everything to do with perspective. Moreover, as we've discovered, perspective is rarely one-sided, but, rather, multi-dimensional, as multi-dimensional as the number of participants in any conversation. To forthrightly answer the question "why," one must delve into the minds and hearts of conversants, to discover what they "know," "feel," and "do"; one must both acknowledge and assess matters of identity and personality, matters of what is basic to culture. And so, I come away from the task of writing this text believing that the undertaking of explaining human language, the "whys" of grammar, is even more daunting than I first imagined. While cut and dried rule-based answers to why this and why that are certainly easier to issue, they are, in reality, least helpful.

The point is that those who are asking the question of "why" are the ones who are desperately trying to fit in somehow, to be successful in life, to flourish in the university classroom and in the wider university community, to fill out a worker's compensation form or obtain a driver's license. The ones asking the question "why" are those who are desirous to put forth a bit effort to help themselves, who are excited about the possibilities and a bit nervous about directly engaging another culture. And while, admittedly, this text cannot possibly address every linguistic context in which a non-native speaker will find him or herself, at least I've given it a try.

So What's Next?

What remains? A great deal, actually. For one thing, how is it that native speakers of English, or any other language for that matter, construct and process linguistic acts (conversation, mainly) with so little difficulty as to seem automatic? What is the exact nature of this neurolinguistic process? We partially know how it happens. From our earliest experiences as babies, language has been modeled for us in its appropriate and varied contexts. And as we grow older, we continue to experience contextualized language which we categorize and interconnect in complex neural networks. It is not that contextualized language happens every now and again; the linguistic notion of "paucity of input" is illusory. To the contrary, contextualized language occurs persistently. It may even be that, in our daily round of activities, we are never without contexts and the language that accompanies them. What remains is to know precisely how context and language are linked in the human brain, the neural-synaptic processes that make these automatic links possible. Unfortunately for those of us who are interested in such questions, neuro-imaging, the tool by which we may discover the secrets of this complex, is still in its formative stages. Neuroscientist Peter Kalivas puts it even more bluntly: "We are all still novices in our understanding of the brain. New discoveries arise every day, but the process is still slow going." One day, perhaps, we may have a better understanding of how the brain does language, and consequently, how we can teach language more efficiently.

Until then, we must be content with viewing that the question of "why" as a question about both the head and the heart. Although it is about what you say and how you say it, it is more about who you are that is enabling. A number of years ago, one of my mentors, a teacher at Union Theological Seminary (who, incidentally, was doing content-based instruction before it was even called that), asked a single question on an exam, "What is effective teaching?" I expounded mightily, giving a thorough answer reflecting the content of the course (after all, it was a course on the philosophy of education). Two weeks or so later, he handed back the exam, and there was no grade. Much to my surprise, he wrote only one sentence: "Now tell me, what do YOU really believe is effective teaching?" I had a eureka moment. He was not asking me about what was in my head. He was asking me about my experience, my motivation, which is the key to unlocking the mystery of "why" for Pedro and for others like him who courageously venture to ask "why."

This handbook is, in large part, a chronicle of how meaning is negotiated; a chronicle of how people use this miraculous yet mundane tool called language to live in fragile harmony together in sometimes fractious communities; a chronicle of two enemies who became friends.

Hazem and Ali entered the ESL program seeking to improve their English so they might return to their countries and build bridges between their respective cultures. The seemingly insurmountable problem was that their cultures were at war. Hazem was from Iraq and Ali from Saudi Arabia. On the night the bombing began, a night filled with surreal images of antiaircraft fire beamed live by satellite on CNN, Ali's brother took to the air in an American-made fighter sold the previous year to the Saudi Air Force to bomb the very Baghdad suburb in which Hazem's family lived. The following day, in the peaceful environs of the university, neither student attended class. I was concerned for both of them and their families, but I learned later that the reason they missed class was so that Ali, whose English was better than Hazem's, could take Hazem to the International Studies Office where he could call his family in Baghdad to make sure they were unharmed by the bombs Ali's brother was dropping on the very same neighborhood. That one act of kindness and friendship made a difference, to Hazem and Ali, to me, to the University of Florida, and to the world.

In an essay on the human family, writer Maya Angelou says:

> Human beings are more alike than unalike, and what is true anywhere is true everywhere, yet I encourage travel to as many destinations as possible for the sake of education as well as pleasure.
>
> A tourist, browsing in a Paris shop, eating in an Italian ristorante, or idling along a Hong Kong street, will encounter three or four languages as she negotiates the buying of a blouse, the paying of a check, or the choosing of a trinket. I do not suggest that simply overhearing a foreign tongue adds to one's understanding of that language. I do know, however, that living exposed to the existence of other languages [and, I might add, other cultures] increases the perception that the world is populated by people who not only speak differently from oneself but whose cultures and philosophies are other than one's own.

Appendix A: Glossary

Amygdala: A complex almond-shaped region in the forebrain having several important functions including the ability to process the emotional meaning of various stimuli.

Anaphora/Anaphoric: In linguistics, a discoursal component which "refers to" something else. A pronoun is anaphoric in that it refers to a noun.

Anterior Cingulate Cortex: A region (cortex) in the frontal lobe which, according to LeDoux, is part of "a cognitive system involved in selective attention, mental resource allocation, decision making processes, and voluntary movement control."[1]

Aspect: In the verbal system, aspect can be defined as the way actions/states behave in discourse. Aspect includes such concepts as sequentiality (sequence of events in time), durativity (how long the actions last), volitionality (actions done on purpose), causation (who or what causes an action to happen), perfectivity (actions which are complete), and object affectedness. (See Tense, Modality, Linearity, Degree of Affectedness, Punctuality and Durativity, Perfective.)

Attitudes: Interpretations of the behavior of persons associated with a particular group or culture.

Binary: A process with only two options. (See Multinary.)

Broca's area: A region of the anterior left hemisphere of the brain considered to be one of the primary regions responsible for syntactic construction. Damage to Broca's area (Broca's Aphasia) disables a person's ability to form well-constructed discourse (agrammatism). Traditional theories concerning the function of Broca's area are being revised given new insights into neural processing. (See Wernicke's area.)

Collective Cultures: Cultures which place high value on the communal nature of society, on the adherence to shared values and behaviors. Collective cultures tend to be high context, and tend toward conformity. (See High Context Culture, Individualist Cultures.)

Common Usage Grammar: The grammar used by speakers of any language as they use that language in everyday speech.

Conditional: A grammatical construction consisting of a subordinate clause and a main clause wherein the focus of the main clause is predicated on truthfulness or possibility of the subordinate clause.

Conditional, Factual: A type of conditional in which the relationship between the two clauses is considered by the speaker immutable. Factual conditionals can be generic or bound by time.

Conditional, Hypothetical: A type of conditional in which the possibility or likelihood of the action of the main clause being fulfilled depends upon the focus of the subordinate clause.

Consciousness: A hotly debated issue in neuroscience, human consciousness, according to Damasio, comprises two fundamental components: a "core consciousness," which enables human beings to be aware of this very moment and this very place; and an "extended consciousness," which evolves over a person's lifetime and includes the complex inter-networking of experience. Extended consciousness allows a person to have an intimate and interconnected relationship between him or herself, the external world and objects and actions in it, and memories of the past coupled with dreams of the future.

Context: The framework or set of circumstances surrounding any event, and by which an event is interpreted linguistically. Context enables perspective.

Convergence Zones: A theory proposed by neuroscientist Antonio Damasio. "Convergence zones located in the prefrontal cortices (see Prefrontal Cortex) are ... the repository of dispositional representations for the appropriately categorized and unique contingencies of our life experiences." Convergence zones are locations wherein representations of varied experiences meet in order to be processed.

Count Nouns: Nouns which can be numerically counted.

Degree of Affectedness: In terms of transitivity, the degree to which the object of an action undergoes that action.

Degree of Specificity: In the Negotiated Perspective of Articles, the degree to which participants in a linguistic event (persons, places and things) are viewed as being specific will largely determine which article (see Determinant), if any, will be used.

Determinants: The linguistic name for articles. Articles are called determinants in as much as they define or determine the specificity and importance of the nouns they modify.

Dialect: The language (pronunciation, morphology, structure) of any particular speech community.

Discourse: The minimal unit of meaning in language. Discourse is any self-contained linguistic event.

Empathy: A representation of the speaker's attitude toward the other participants, which can be people or things, in an event. Point of view or camera angles.

Ends: Goals of a culture which justify its existence.

Ethnocentrism: The view that one's culture is the center of the universe.

Focus: Referring to point of view. (See Empathy.)

Grammar of Literacy: Grammatical conventions created and assigned for reading and writing.

High Context Culture: A means of defining how members of a culture communicate. In a high context culture, the context is not included in the linguistic code. High context language is viewed as being indirect and inexplicit. (See Low Context Culture.)

Illocutionary Force: An illocutionary speech act is one in which an action is accomplished by saying something. Illocutionary speech acts can be direct or indirect. For example, by saying, "I now pronounce you husband and wife," a marriage is performed. "Gee, don't you think it's hot in here?" functions as an indirect way of asking someone to open a window.

Immediacy: In manipulative speech acts, the extent to which the speaker (manipulator) intends the act to be carried out quickly.

Individualist Cultures: Cultures which place a high emphasis on the uniqueness and independence of individuals within a community, as opposed to collective cultures, which place high value on the collective, on the adherence to shared values and behaviors.

Intentionality: In human communication, intention refers to the purpose or goal of any interaction.

Interlocutor: A participant in a linguistic act, whether it be conversational or an act of literacy (reading and writing).

Intransitive: A verb which cannot carry a direct object.

Limbic System: In traditional neuroscientific terms, "a circle of connections that mediates emotion" (see LeDoux's refutation, 1996:99). The Limbic System is located between the hypothalamus and the neocortex and is one of many areas that involve some emotional and cognitive processes.

Linearity: Involving sequential action in time.

Low Context Culture: A means of defining how members of a culture communicate. In a low context culture, the context is included in the linguistic code. Low context language is viewed as being direct and explicit.

Manipulatives: Speech acts which have as their goal to change an established norm or the status quo.

Mass Nouns: Non-countable nouns conceived more concretely than other more-abstract non-count nouns (beer vs. hope).

Means: Defined by Gudykunst and Kim as that which constitutes acceptable behavior within a particular society or cultural group.

Modality: Celce-Murcia and Larsen-Freeman (1999) define modals as "tenseless auxiliaries that take no subject-verb agreement and no infinitive 'to' before the following verb.[2] Modality involves such functional notions as possibility, ability, desire, preference, and offer.

Monochronic Time: The cultural notion of time in which members of a culture do one thing at a time.

Morphology: An area of linguistics that analyzes the minimal unit of grammatical form.

Motivational Valence: In the theory of Negotiated Perspective, Motivational Valence consists of a complex set of variables, including the degree to which an individual is motivated to communicate and the degree of emotional involvement in the event which prompts the linguistic act.

Multinary: Something which is binary has only two options, usually on or off; that is, it either is or is not. A process which is "multinary" has many options. That grammar is multinary means that speakers have many syntactic options to express a particular intention.

Negotiated Perspective: The pragmatic variables which speakers use to co-construct meaning in communication differ from context to context. Even within the same context, speakers may approach communication with different experiences and a different understanding of the context. Since language, and specifically grammatical form, is the means by which perspective is co-constructed or negotiated, and since perspectives may indeed be different, there is a certain unpredictability in communication. Negotiated Perspective is the means by which unpredictability in communication becomes predictable.

Neurolinguistics: A branch of linguistics dedicated to the study of the construction and processing of language in the brain.

Passive: One of the "voices" in English grammar. A passive is formed by placing the direct object of a transitive verb in subject position, using a *be*, *have* or *get* auxiliary plus the past participle of the main verb — Sally kissed Max is active, but Max was kissed is passive. Passives are used when the speakers wants to emphasize the undergoer of the action of the verb (the direct object).

Perfective: Verbal aspect in which actions have been completed, and those actions are important at the time of the linguistic act.

Polychronic Time: The culturally-influenced ability to do many things at one time.

Potentiality: In grammar, a process having potential.

Pragmatics: In linguistic analysis, pragmatics involves such issues as intention, presupposition (assumptions made by speakers about what hearers will accept without challenge), implicature (what is implied apart from what is said), inference (using background knowledge/experience to interpret discourse), reference, and context.

Prefrontal Cortex: A region of the brain directly behind the frontal cortex involved in the most sophisticated cognitive functions human beings perform. The prefrontal cortex plays a significant role in planning, prioritizing, prediction and choosing from among options. Regions of the prefrontal cortex may be linked with the amygdala to perform emotional processes.

Prescriptivism: A set of carefully defined rules guiding the use and function of grammar.

Progressive: A type of grammatical aspect which focuses on actions which are ongoing. These continuing actions can be in the past, present or future.

Prohibitive: A type of speech act, specifically, a type of second-person command which disallows the hearer from accomplishing the action of the verb.

Punctuality and Durativity: A term used to define the degree to which a verb which takes an object is transitive. Punctual actions occur quickly with little time transpiring between when the action began and when it ended. Durative actions, by contrast, occur with some time transpiring between the inception of the action and the action's completion.

Referential: In language, a pronoun which refers to someone known by both the speaker and hearer.

Scalar: On a gradable scale (having many options) as opposed to being binary (having only two options).

Semantics: The study of meaning in language.

Spatiality: Dimensions of space expressed in language. Prepositional phrases, such as *on the table* in the expression *the book is on the table*, communicate the location of an object in space.

Speech Act: Language performance or discourse used to "do" something in a particular context. In its broadest terms, a speech act encompasses all of language. Simply saying something, as well as questioning, commanding, making promises, warning, etc., are considered speech acts.

Stative: A type of verb which expresses a condition of being, as in "The earth is round." These states of being can be fixed or mutable.

Stereoscopic: The ability to view persons, concepts and actions in three dimensions.

Stereotypes: Categorizations of certain groups of people, such as racial or ethnic groups, based solely upon the behaviors of a few members of that group.

Subjunctive: A type of hypothetical conditional used when there is little possibility that the condition will be fulfilled. The subjunctive is dream language, as in "If I were a millionaire, I would buy a Porsche." The subjunctive can also be used as a command form, as in "If I were you, I'd..."

Syntax: The linear component structure of language.

Tense: Refers to time, especially as it relates to actions.

Transitive: In the expression, "Sam kissed Sally," the verb *to kiss* is considered transitive because it can take a direct object. Linguists point out that there are degrees of transitivity depending upon such issues as the degree to which the object is affected by the action of the verb and the degree to which the action is punctual or durative (see above).

Values: The enduring and essential beliefs of any community of people. Some define a value as any belief a community will fight vigorously to maintain.

Videoscopic: The ability to view persons, concepts and actions over a particular span of time.

Wernicke's Area: A region of the left hemisphere in most people near the junction of the temporal and parietal lobes, near the primary auditory cortex. Wernicke's area is considered to be one of the regions responsible for semantic meaning in both the processing and construction of discourse. Damage to Wernicke's area (Wernicke's Aphasia) disables a person's ability to construct coherent discourse. Speech production is commonly grammatical, but makes little semantic sense. Traditional theories concerning the function of Wernicke's area are being revised given new insights into neural processing.

World View: The process whereby members of a culture interpret the larger context of their world. World view encompasses cultural values, societal goals and expected behaviors.

Appendix B: Internet Resources

The resources listed below are selected from literally hundreds of websites catering to teachers of English as a second or foreign language. While this text primarily covers the grammar of common usage, the websites listed below, and categorized according to general topic, have been selected to give the ESL/EFL teacher and student a wide range of resources in a variety of areas essential to success in the classroom. **The sites chosen are free to students and teachers.**

Professional Resources for Teachers
(Including resources for careers in TESL/TEFL)

- http://www.tesol.org/s_tesol/index.asp The official website of the largest and most prestigious organization of ESL/EFL teachers.
- http://www.caslt.org/ The Canadian Association of Second Language Teachers has a plethora of materials on its website for teachers of ESL/EFL.
- http://www.matesol.info/ For those searching for MA programs in TESL/TESL/Applied Linguistics, this website offers links to universities worldwide.
- http://www.eslcafe.com/ One of the oldest and most popular sites for ESL/EFL teachers. Dave's site has links to classroom activities as well as jobs in the field.
- http://www.eslbase.com/ This helpful website specializes in job listings in ESL/EFL worldwide and features discussion groups on a variety of issues from classroom activities to language acquisition and grammar.
- http://eff.cls.utk.edu/toolkit/default.htm An adult ESL education website designed to enable the teacher to design and complete a standards-based curriculum.

Language Acquisition/Linguistics Resources

- http://www.cal.org/ The Center for Applied Linguistics has a number of resources online dealing with language acquisition and the linguistic theory behind the teaching of ESL/EFL.

- http://www.cal.org/caela/ Center for Applied Linguistics resources for the adult learner.
- http://linguistlist.org/ A popular website for linguists and those interested in linguistics. It features an "Ask A Linguist" link where questions are asked and answered (or at least attempted).

ACTIVITIES FOR TEACHERS AND STUDENTS OF ESL/EFL

The websites below offer many interesting English learning activities for students of all ages and at all proficiency levels.

- http://www.english-daily.com/
- http://www.welcometoenglishandfun.com/
- http://www.tolearnenglish.com/
- http://www.esl4teachers.com/
- http://www.esl-galaxy.com/
- http://www.eslgold.com/
- http://www.5minuteenglish.com/resources/esl-quizzes-lesson-plans-activities.html
- http://iteslj.org/
- http://www.real-english.com/

GRAMMAR ACTIVITIES FOR TEACHERS OF ESL/EFL

- http://www.english-the-easy-way.com/ English The Easy Way is an excellent resource for college-level writing and the grammatical conventions for effective writing.
- http://a4esl.org/a/g.html Offers a number of grammar quizzes of varying difficulty. The quizzes are separated by topic.
- http://www.edufind.com/english/grammar/grammar_topics.php A resource with discussions and quizzes on various aspects of grammar. Registration is required but free.
- http://grammar.ccc.commnet.edu/grammar/quiz_list.htm Another site offering interactive grammar quizzes.
- http://web2.uvcs.uvic.ca/elc/studyzone/330/grammar/index.htm This site, maintained by the University of Victoria (Canada), contains detailed explanations of a variety of grammatical topics as well as exercises for practice.

REFERENCE RESOURCES (DICTIONARIES, ETC.)

- http://www.learnersdictionary.com/ The online Merriam-Webster's Dictionary of English. Registration is required but the site is free for registrants.

- http://www.ldoceonline.com/ The Longman English Dictionary online. A very popular dictionary for teachers and students of ESL/EFL.
- http://www.esldesk.com/ The ESL Deck is a comprehensive website with links to grammar, vocabulary and spelling activities. There are also links to ESL teacher-training programs as well as scholarships.
- http://en.bab.la/phrases/ A helpful phrase dictionary allowing the user to translate common phrases into several languages.
- http://www.wordreference.com/ Another very helpful site allowing the user to translate phrases between several languages. Slang expressions are also included.
- http://www.soundsofenglish.org/ A resource for teachers and students describing in detail how the sounds of English are constructed in the vocal tract.
- http://www.ets.org/toefl Educational Testing Service online provides information for students planning to take the Test of English as a Foreign Language.

Notes

Introduction
1. Zucker 2006: 3920.

Chapter 1
1. The title of the chapter, as well as the title of the theory itself, Mascagni Effect, is my invention. It represents a twofold thought; first, that language and musical competence are interrelated (n.b.: competence here does not necessarily correspond to one's proficiency to read music nor the ability to play a musical instrument); and second, that meaning in language is related to one's perspective as shaped through experience.
2. Foucault 1969; Foucault 1970.
3. Presently, Dr. Antonio Damasio is the David Dornsife Professor of Neuroscience at the University of Southern California as well as the Director of the University's Brain and Creativity Institute.
4. This quote is taken from Cara Ernst's final examination in Second Language Acquisition. In this text, I have used the results of many students' research.
5. Ratey 2002.
6. Damasio 1994: 182.
7. Calvin and Ojemann: 1995.
8. J. Austin 1999: 358.
9. Gudykunst and Kim: 1997.
10. M. Ward.
11. Lakoff 1987; Turner 1996.
12. Kuno and Kaburaki .
13. Kalivas. Personal communication. Professor Kalivas was my mentor during my sabbatical leave at the Medical University of South Carolina in Charleston.
14. Bill Wilson is an associate professor of music emeritus at Appalachian State University. He has been a most valuable resource in assisting me to frame my theory that the acquisition of language and the acquisition of music are intimately intertwined, a theory quite contrary to those that espouse the computational nature of language.

Chapter 2
1. Gudykunst and Kim 1997.
2. Givon 1984.
3. The pyramid model is based on an essay written by a team of graduate students, Rob Jolly, Mary Farthing, and Beth Wooten, during the summer intensive TESL training program in 1997.

4. The idea to represent the function of articles in common-usage English was suggested by Veronica Lozano Toub, and is thus named the Lozano Continuum in her honor.

5. This conversation actually occurred. While I was not one of the interlocutors, I was a part of the conversation.

Chapter 3

1. The Grammar Book has an extensive discussion of the common uses of English prepositions.
2. Turner 1996: 13.
3. Turner 1996: 15.
4. Turner 1996: 17.
5. Turner 1996: 17.

Chapter 4

1. *American Heritage Book of English Usage* 1996.
2. Celce-Murcia and Larsen-Freeman 1983: 345.

Chapter 5

1. The Bolinger Principle, as it became widely known, was first expressed in a 1968 article in *Glossa* titled "Entailment and the Meaning of Structures." Its full expression came in his book *Meaning and Form*. To this day, the Bolinger Principle remains perhaps the most robust theory of the way gerunds and infinitives work in English.
2. Robinson 1995.
3. Bladon 1968.

Chapter 7

1. J.L. Austin 1951.
2. Searle 1969.
3. Honderich 1995: 489.
4. Givon 1993.
5. Givon 1993.
6. *American Tongues* is an hour-long video that takes the viewer on a journey though the various dialects of the United States.
7. Tannen 2001.

Chapter 9

1. Celce-Murcia and Larsen-Freeman 1984.
2. *American Tongues*.

Chapter 11

1. Celce-Murcia and Larsen-Freeman 1983: 315.
2. Celce-Murcia and Larsen-Freeman 1983: 316.

Appendix A

1. Ledoux 1998: 277.
2. Celce-Murcia and Larsen-Freeman 1983: 138.

Annotated Bibliography

American Heritage Book of English Usage. New York: Houghton Mifflin, 1996.

American Tongues. Produced and directed by L. Alvarez and A. Kolker. Center for New American Media, 1986. An entertaining hour-long video that takes the viewer on a dialectal journey across the United States. Some of the more interesting features are: features of regional dialects and differences between them, prejudice against certain dialects, African-American vernacular English, obscure but interesting dialects like that of Tangier Island, Virginia.

Angelou, M. *Wouldn't Take Nothing for My Journey Now*. New York: Random House, 1993. This volume of Maya Angelou's short, poignant essays and reflections tackles many of life's enduring issues.

Antonio, Juliano Desiderato. "Functionalism and Textual Linguistics Contributions for Teaching Grammar at School." *Acta Scientiarum: Human and Social Sciences* 27.1 (2005): 1–6. *CSA Linguistics and Language Behavior Abstracts*. Web. 14 June 2010.

Austin, J. *Zen and the Brain*. Cambridge, MA: MIT Press, 1999.

Austin, J.L. *How to Do Things with Words*. Oxford: Oxford University Press, 1951.

Baricevic, Emina. "Dialectal Speech in Teaching Grammar." *Ucitelj* 5 (2005): 113–8. *CSA Linguistics and Language Behavior Abstracts*. Web. 14 June 2010.

Bladon, R.A.W. "Selecting the to- or -ing Nominal after Like, Love, Hate, Dislike and Prefer." *English Studies* 49 (1968): 203–214.

Bolinger, D. "Entailment and the Meaning of Structures." *Glossa* 2 (Summer 1968): 119–127.

———. *Meaning and Form*. London: Longman Higher Education, 1977.

Borg, Simon. "Teacher Cognition in Grammar Teaching: A Literature Review." *Language Awareness* 12.2 (2003): 96–108. *CSA Linguistics and Language Behavior Abstracts*. Web. 14 June 2010.

Borg, Simon, and Anne Burns. "Integrating Grammar in Adult TESOL Classrooms." *Applied Linguistics* 29.3 (2008): 456–82. *CSA Linguistics and Language Behavior Abstracts*. Web. 14 June 2010.

Braun, A.R., A. Guillemin, L. Hosey, and M. Varga. "The Neural Organization of Discourse." *Brain* 124, No. 10 (October 2001): 2028–2044.

Calvin, C., and G. Ojemann. *Conversations with Neil's Brain: The Neural Nature of Thought and Language*. New York: Basic Books, 1995.

Caplan, R., and M. Dapretto. "Making Sense During Conversation." *Neuroreport* 12, No. 16 (November 16, 2001): 3625–3632.

Celce-Murcia, M., and D. Larsen-Freeman. *The Grammar Book: An ESL/EFL Teacher's Course*, 2d ed. Thomson Learning, 1999. Grammatical descriptions and teaching suggestions are organized into sections dealing with form, meaning and use. It helps teachers and future teachers grasp the linguistic system and details of English grammar, providing more information on how structures are used at the discourse level. This book has been the gold standard ESL grammar text for many years. The grammatical explanations in the text are more useful for writing. Students who have used this text have commented that it is overwhelming, and that it is expensive.

Chafe, W. *Discourse, Consciousness, and Time.* Chicago: University of Chicago Press, 1994.

Chierchia, G. "Topics in the Syntax and Semantics of Infinitives and Gerunds." *Dissertation Abstracts International* 45 (July 1984): 168A.

Chomsky, N. *Aspects of the Theory of Syntax.* Cambridge, MA: MIT Press, 1965.

_____. *Language and Mind.* Rev. ed. New York: Harcourt Brace Jovanovich, 1972.

_____. *Some Concepts and Consequences of the Theory of Government and Binding.* Cambridge, MA: MIT Press, 1982.

_____. *Syntactic Structures.* The Hague: Mouton Publishers, 1957. Professor Chomsky has been, arguably, the premiere linguistic theorist of the twentieth century. His 1957 work, cited here, gave rise to a new way of conceiving human language, as an innate module of the human mind/brain with universal principles shared by all languages, what he termed "Universal Grammar." His theories have undergone changes over the four decades they have been reviewed and debated.

Cullen, Richard. "Teaching Grammar as a Liberating Force." *ELT Journal* 62.3 (2008): 221–30. *CSA Linguistics and Language Behavior Abstracts.* Web. 14 June 2010.

Damasio, A. *Descartes' Error.* New York: Gossett/Putnam, 1994. Dr. Damasio is a neurologist and the David Dornsife Professor of Neuroscience at the University of Southern California. He serves as Director USC's Brain and Creativity Institute and Adjunct Professor at the Salk Institute. Professor Damasio has shown that emotion has a neural basis. He attempts to explain the neurophysiology of human emotion, language, and cognition. The three works cited here have won numerous awards.

_____. *The Feeling of What Happens: Body and Emotion on the Making of Consciousness.* Orlando, FL: Harcourt, 1999.

_____. *Finding Spinoza.* Orlando, FL: Harcourt, 2003.

Davis, Joseph. "Rule and Meaning in the Teaching of Grammar." *Language and Linguistics Compass* 3.1 (2009): 199–221. *CSA Linguistics and Language Behavior Abstracts.* Web. 14 June 2010.

Davy, B. "A Cognitive-Semantic Approach to the Acquisition of English Prepositions." *Dissertation Abstracts International* 61, No. 12 (June 2001): 4750.

Doran, Nicholas. "Practical English Language Teaching: Grammar." *JALT Journal* 29.2 (2007): 252–4. *CSA Linguistics and Language Behavior Abstracts.* Web. 14 June 2010.

Ferstl, E.C., and D.Y. von Cramon. "What Does the Frontomedian Cortex Contribute to Language Processing?: A Coherence Theory of Mind." *Neuroimage* 3 (November 17, 2002): 599–612.

Foucault, M. *L'Archéologie du savoir.* Paris: Éditions Gallimard. 1969. This work by Foucault defines how discourse functions. Discourse is comprised of "statements." Statements are what determine the meaningfulness of speech. In his theory, statements are dependent upon the context from which they arise. A particular statement is dependent upon what precedes it and what follows it, thus, upon the context of the entire discourse.

_____. *The Order of Things.* New York: Pantheon, 1970. One of Michel Foucault's seminal works. In it, he defines discourse as the underlying truths held by communities/cultures at various times. This discourse changes through time, sometimes rapidly.

Freedle, R.O. "Advances in discourse processing." In *Discourse in Society: Systemic Functional Perspectives (Meaning and Choice in Language: Studies for Michael Halliday).* P.H. Fries and M. Gregory, eds. Volume L. Norwood, NJ: Ablex, 1995.

Givón, T. *English Grammar.* Philadelphia: John Benjamins, 1993.

_____. *Syntax: A Functional-Typological Introduction.* Philadelphia: John Benjamins, 1984. Professor Givon's contributions to the field of functional syntax are great. In the two works cited here he delves deeply into the structure of language grammar (including that of English), and how grammar functions in enabling or disabling human communication.

Gladwell, M. *Blink.* New York: Little, Brown, 2005.

Gray, J., T. Brauer, and M. Raichle. "Integration of Emotion and Cognition in the Lateral Prefrontal Cortex." *PNAS* 99 (2002): 4115–4120.

Grice, H.P. "Logic and Conversation." In *Syntax and Semantics*. Vol. 3. P. Cole and J. Morgan, eds. New York: Academic Press, 1975.
Gudykunst, W., and Y. Kim. *Communicating with Strangers: An Approach to Intercultural Communication*. New York: Random House, 1997.
Gupta, Deepti. "Teaching Grammar Creatively." *ELT Journal* 62.4 (2008): 424–7. CSA Linguistics and Language Behavior Abstracts. Web. 14 June 2010.
Hasan, R. "The Conception of Context in Text." In *Discourse in Society: Systemic Functional Perspectives*. P.H. Fries and M. Gregory, eds. Norwood, NJ: Ablex, 1995.
Hellen, L. "On the Logical Form of Infinitives and Gerunds." *Cahiers linguistiques d'Ottawa* 9 (1980): 191–212.
Honderich, T., ed. *The Oxford Companion to Philosophy*. Oxford: Oxford University Press, 1995.
Human Connectome Project Home. 24 September 2010. 19 October 2010. http://humanconnectome.org/.
Kalivas, P.W., N. Volkow, and J. Seamans. "Unmanageable Motivation in Addiction: A Pathology in Prefrontal-Accumbens Glutamate Transmission." *Neuron* 45 (March 3, 2005): 647–650.
Kandel, E., J. Schwartz, and T. Jessell. *Essentials of Neural Science and Behavior*. New York: McGraw-Hill, 1995.
Kettle, Margaret. "Teaching English as Discourse: A Challenge for the ELICOS Classroom." *EA Journal* 17.2 (2000): 66–77. CSA Linguistics and Language Behavior Abstracts. Web. 14 June 2010.
Kolb, B., and I. Whishaw. *Fundamentals of Human Neuropsychology*. New York: Worth Publishers, 2003. An insightful textbook on the interplay between neurophysiology and human psychology.
Kuno, S., and E. Kaburaki. "Empathy and Syntax." *Linguistic Inquiry* 8 (1977): 627–72.
Lakoff, G. *Women, Fire and Dangerous Things: What Categories Reveal About the Mind*. Chicago: University of Chicago Press, 1987.
LeDoux, J. *The Emotional Brain*. New York: Touchstone, 1996. Professor Ledoux's work on the brain.
———. *The Synaptic Brain*. New York: Penguin, 2002.
Lemke, Jay. "Intertextuality and Text Semantics." In *Discourse in Society: Systemic Functional Perspectives*. P.H. Fries and M. Gregory, eds. Norwood, NJ: Ablex, 1995.
Leslie, K.R., S.H. Johnson-Frey, and S.T. Grafton. "Functional Imaging of Face and Hand Imitation: Towards a Motor Theory of Empathy." *Neuroimage* 2 (February 21, 2004): 601–607.
Lukin, Annabelle. "Functional Grammar and Dictagloss: What Does 'Good Grammar' Really Mean?" *TESOL in Context* 4.2 (1994): 49–51. CSA Linguistics and Language Behavior Abstracts. Web. 14 June 2010.
McGarry, R. *The Subtle Slant: A Cross-Linguistic Discourse Analysis Model for Evaluating Interethnic Conflict in the Press*. Boone, North Carolina: Parkway, 1994.
McHoul, A., and W. Grace. *A Foucault Primer: Discourse, Power and the Subject*. New York: New York University Press, 1997.
Merleau-Ponty, M. *Consciousness and the Acquisition of Language*. Evanston, Ill.: Northwestern University Press, 1973. Influenced by Heidegger, Marx and Husserl, Merleau-Ponty elucidates how one's perception, resulting from active engagement in the world, influences one's understanding of the world. According to Merleau-Ponty, language is the center of our understanding of culture. He is often credited as being a leading influence of what is termed "Post Cognitivism."
Mishra, Prashant. "Challenges and Problems in the Teaching of Grammar." *Language in India* 10.2 (2010): 175–87. CSA Linguistics and Language Behavior Abstracts. Web. 14 June 2010.
Nassaji, Hossein, and Sandra Fotos. "Current Developments in Research on the Teaching of Grammar." *Annual Review of Applied Linguistics* 24 (2004): 126–45. CSA Linguistics and Language Behavior Abstracts. Web. 14 June 2010.
Newman, S.D., M.A. Just, and P.A. Carpenter. "The Synchronization of the Human Cortical Working Memory Network." *Neuroimage* 4 (April 15, 2002): 810–822.

Opitz, B., A. Mecklinger, and A. Friederics. "Functional Asymmetry of the Human Prefrontal Cortex: Encoding and Retrieval of Verbally and Non-Verbally Encoded Information." *Learning and Memory* 7, No. 2 (March/April 2000): 85–96.

Pawlak, Miroslaw. "On the Effectiveness of Options in Grammar Teaching: Translating Theory and Research into Classroom Practice." *Studia Anglica Posnaniensia* 40 (2004): 269–87. *CSA Linguistics and Language Behavior Abstracts*. Web. 14 June 2010.

Portner, P. "Gerunds and Types of Events." *Cornell Working Papers in Linguistics* 10 (Fall 1991): 189–208.

Pullam, G. "English Nominal Gerund Phrases as Noun Phrases with Verb Phrase Heads. In *Who Climbs the Grammar Tree?* R. Tracy, ed. Tubingen: Niemeyer, 1992.

Ratey, J. *A User's Guide to the Brain: Perception, Attention, and the Four Theaters of the Brain*. New York: Vintage, 2002. An interesting work that introduces the reader to the complex processes of the human brain. In this book, Professor Ratey, who is a professor of psychiatry at Harvard Medical School, discusses how the brain develops, how that development can be stunted by substances such as cocaine and tobacco, and how humans perceive the world through their senses, attention, and consciousness.

Richardson, A. "A Grammatical Description of the English Gerund and Related Forms." *Dissertation Abstracts International* 52 (May 1992): 3910A.

Robinson, B. *Focus: Interactive Grammar for Students of ESL*. 2nd ed. New York: St. Martin's Press, 1995. Does a credible job contextualizing gerunds and infinitives, but the contexts can seem contrived. Little in the teaching activities is based on enabling students to make appropriate choices in the wide variety of situations they face daily in real-time communication.

Schachter, P. "A Non-Transformational Account of Gerundive Nominals in English." *Linguistic Inquiry* 7, No. 2 (1976): 205–241.

Searle, J. *Speech Acts*. Cambridge: Cambridge University Press, 1969.

Shapiro, K.A., et al. "Grammatical Distinctions in the Left Frontal Cortex." *Journal of Cognitive Neuroscience* 13 (2001): 713–720.

Sperber, D., and D. Wilson. *Relevance*. Cambridge, MA: Harvard University Press, 1995.

Tannen, D. *Talking 9 to 5: Women and Men at Work*. New York: Quill, 2001. Professor Tannen's important research on the conversational styles, language and gender, and multi-generational conversation has changed the way we understand communication between men and women, and between women and their daughters. Only two of her works are cited here, but other books of interest are: *You Were Always Mom's Favorite: Sisters in Conversation Throughout Their Lives* (2010), *You're Wearing THAT?* (2006), and *I Only Say This Because I Love You* (2002)

———. *You Just Don't Understand: Women and Men in Conversation*. New York: Quill, 2001.

Thompson, R. *The Brain: A Neuroscience Primer*. 3rd ed. New York: Worth Publishers, 2000.

Turner, Mark. *The Literary Mind*. New York: Oxford University Press, 1996. This work changed my way of thinking about "text." Professor Turner argues that "storying" and projecting stories onto other stories, what he calls "parable," lie at the heart of human perception, and thus have a vital role to play in our understanding of how language is created and understood.

Wu, Y. "Analysis of Strategies on Higher Verbs and Their Non-Finite Complements." *RELC Journal* 23, No. 2 (1992): 35–43.

Zucker, Connie K. "Teaching Grammar in the Foreign Language Classroom: A Study of Teacher Beliefs, Teacher Practices, and Current Research." *CSA Linguistics and Language Behavior Abstracts*. Web. 14 June 2010.

Index

a 51; *see also* indefinite article
above 9
acquisition 17
adverbial phrases 140
adverbials 140
ain't 115, 116
ambihemispheric 17
American Heritage Book of English Usage 83
American Tongues 115, 135, 172
an 51
anaphoric 56
anterior cingulate gyrus 17
Appalachia 32
Appalachian State University 109, 113, 136, 157, 171
Applied English Grammar 3
articles 3, 45, 49, 50, 51, 52, 54, 55, 56, 57, 58, 60, 91, 145, 162, 172
aspect 33, 35, 46, 79, 107, 161, 164, 165
association cortices 19
attitudes 25, 26, 50, 121
Austin, James 18
Austin, J.L. 110

BE passive *see* passives
binary 41, 43, 70, 84, 103, 155, 164, 165
Blink 7
bodies of knowledge 15
Bolinger, Dwight 105
Bolinger Principle 97
Borg, Simon 7
boundedness 67
Broca's area 11
Burns, Anna 7

can 2, 3, 6, 10, 11, 13, 14, 15, 17, 19, 20, 24, 25, 26, 27, 28, 32, 34, 35, 36, 40, 41, 42, 45, 47, 49, 50, 51, 52, 56, 58, 59, 65, 66, 67, 68, 74, 75, 76, 77, 79, 80, 81, 85, 86, 87, 88, 91, 92, 93, 94, 95, 96, 100, 103, 104, 110, 111, 112, 113, 114, 115, 118, 120, 122, 126, 129, 130, 131, 132, 133, 135, 136, 137, 140, 146, 154, 155, 157, 158, 159, 161, 162, 163, 165, 166
Carte de Séjour 42
Cavalleria Rusticana 36, 37
Celce-Murcia, Marianne 3, 132
Charlotte Observer 7, 61
Chiapas 156, 157
China 49, 51, 79, 83
Chomsky, Noam 11
cohortative 31, 32
collective 29
communication 7
context 3, 6, 7, 8, 9, 11, 13, 14, 15, 17, 20, 23, 27, 28, 34, 37, 38, 40, 42, 43, 44, 45, 47, 50, 51, 52, 57, 59, 60, 61, 79, 82, 85, 89, 96, 97, 98, 100, 101, 102, 110, 113, 114, 122, 123, 132, 133, 134, 144, 145, 151, 153, 155, 159, 161, 163, 164, 165, 166, 174
contextualized communication 20
convergence zones 18, 23
Cooke, Austin 144
Cullen, Richard 8
cultural variables 24
culture 2, 5, 10, 11, 20, 23, 24, 27, 32, 38, 39, 40, 41, 42, 43, 44, 45, 46, 50, 51, 58, 61, 80, 82, 83, 85, 86, 87, 88, 110, 112, 113, 121, 123, 134, 135, 137, 139, 157, 158, 159, 161, 163, 164, 166, 175

Damasio, Antonio 17, 18, 162, 171
declarative memory 17
definite article 52
definiteness 52
determiners 49
D.I.P.P.S. 22
discoordination 30
discoursal scaffold 27
discourse 5, 7, 9, 12, 15, 16, 19, 23, 27, 28,

178 Index

29, 30, 31, 35, 37, 40, 43, 44, 45, 47, 48, 50, 51, 52, 63, 69, 79, 89, 90, 95, 96, 97, 98, 102, 106, 108, 110, 115, 116, 117, 122, 128, 132, 152, 155, 161, 164, 165, 166
Disney World 93, 94, 109
D.O.M.P.S 22
double modals 135, 136

l'embrouillement de la langue 41
empathy 34, 162, 163
English 2, 3, 5, 6, 9, 10, 13, 19, 21, 22, 31, 32, 33, 42, 45, 46, 47, 49, 51, 52, 55, 57, 58, 59, 60, 62, 64, 66, 67, 70, 73, 74, 79, 80, 82, 83, 88, 90, 95, 96, 97, 99, 106, 107, 109, 118, 119, 120, 124, 125, 130, 132, 136, 139, 140, 148, 149, 150, 152, 153, 155, 156, 157, 158, 159, 160, 164, 167, 168, 169, 172, 174, 176
Environmental Variables 26
event 34
experience 37

Farthing, Mary 54
Fiddler on the Roof 85
fMRI 19
Foucault, Michel 15, 174
France 12, 15, 18, 38, 39, 42, 43, 44, 45, 46, 47, 49, 52, 53, 54, 56, 57, 62, 70, 82, 83, 84, 85, 148

gender 25, 45, 46, 47, 136
generative grammar 107
Germany 60
gerunds 3, 22, 23, 36, 91, 92, 93, 94, 95, 96, 97, 98, 100, 101, 102, 103, 104, 106, 172
GET passive *see* passives
Givon, Tom 52, 113, 120
Gladwell, Malcolm 6
glucocorticoids 19
Godfather III 37
grammar 2, 3, 5, 6, 7, 8, 9, 11, 12, 13, 18, 20, 21, 23, 27, 32, 33, 36, 38, 40, 56, 60, 83, 91, 92, 96, 101, 103, 106, 107, 110, 120, 125, 130, 131, 132, 149, 150, 153, 154, 155, 156, 158, 161, 164, 165, 167, 168, 169
The Grammar Book 3
Gudykunst, William 23, 24, 25, 50, 51, 171
Gulfstream 121, 122

have passives *see* passives
Hawkins, Kelly 136
high context cultures 50
hippocampus 18
hybridized perspective 11

if I were you 88, 114, 122, 165
illocutionary 110, 111, 163

image schema 75
imperatives 3, 35, 112, 120, 121, 123
in 2; *see also* prepositions
indefinite article 52, 152
indicative 31, 35, 84
infinitives 3, 6, 22, 23, 36, 91, 92, 93, 94, 95, 96, 97, 98, 100, 101, 102, 103, 104, 106, 164, 172
interlocutors 9, 28, 35, 40, 48, 70, 97, 110, 123, 146, 172
interrogatives 3, 35, 112, 116, 119, 123

Japan 10, 51, 66, 67, 79, 83, 91, 112, 113
Jolly, Robb 54

Kaburaki 34, 171
Kalivas, Peter 35, 159
Kettle, Margaret 8
Kilpatrick, James 5
Kim, Young Yun 23, 24, 25, 50, 51, 171
knowledge of the world 28
Kuno, Susumu 34

L2 40, 41, 43, 45, 46, 47
Lakoff, George 34
language 5
Larsen-Freeman, Diane 3, 132
like death warmed over 75
limbic system 17
Limp Bizkit 115, 117
linguistic discourse 8
The Literary Mind 74
locutionary 110
long-term memory 17, 40
long-term potentiation (LTP) 18, 19, 21
low context culture 50

macro-level discourse 15
Maine et La Loire 44
manipulative speech acts 109, 112, 122, 163
manipulatives 35
Mascagni 9, 36, 37, 38, 59, 61, 108, 171
The Mascagni Effect 9
mass noun 58
may 2, 5, 6, 18, 19, 20, 23, 27, 28, 34, 36, 38, 39, 40, 41, 42, 44, 45, 46, 49, 50, 51, 56, 57, 60, 64, 68, 69, 74, 75, 76, 79, 83, 84, 88, 89, 95, 96, 100, 102, 104, 113, 114, 115, 116, 117, 120, 121, 122, 125, 130, 131, 132, 133, 134, 135, 136, 137, 141, 145, 146, 153, 158, 159, 164, 165; *see also* prepositions
Medical University of South Carolina 35, 171
metaphor 29, 32, 40, 74
modality 33, 35, 89, 107, 133, 134
modeling 7, 24, 92, 130, 131, 132, 137

Mondrian, Piet 93
mood 35, 84
motivation 45
motivational valence 35, 36, 95, 101, 164
Museum of Modern Art 93

Narbonne 38, 44
narrative imaging 32, 68, 74
negation 113, 115, 122
negotiated perspective 28, 29, 31, 32, 48, 55, 62, 64, 66, 69, 74, 90, 92, 106, 134, 162, 164
North Carolina 20, 27, 61, 111, 136, 141, 150, 156, 157

Ojemann, George 19
on 2, 5, 6, 9, 10, 11, 12, 13, 15, 16, 17, 18, 20, 21, 22, 23, 24, 25, 26, 28, 30, 31, 32, 33, 34, 35, 36, 37, 38, 39, 40, 42, 44, 46, 47, 50, 52, 53, 57, 58, 59, 61, 62, 64, 65, 66, 67, 69, 74, 75, 76, 77, 79, 80, 82, 83, 84, 85, 86, 87, 88, 90, 91, 92, 93, 94, 95, 96, 97, 98, 100, 101, 102, 103, 104, 106, 107, 109, 110, 111, 112, 113, 114, 115, 116, 117, 118, 119, 120, 121, 122, 123, 124, 126, 127, 128, 130, 131, 132, 133, 134, 135, 136, 137, 138, 139, 140, 141, 144, 145, 146, 149, 152, 153, 156, 157, 158, 159, 160, 161, 162, 163, 164, 165, 167, 168, 171, 172

Pájaro, Victor 118
parable 75
Paris 34, 53, 160, 174
passives 124, 125, 164
Pembrotanck University 13, 80, 94, 127, 128
Perez-Reverte, Arturo 69
perlocutionary 111
perspective 10, 11, 28, 29, 31, 32, 33, 35, 36, 37, 41, 43, 47, 48, 57, 69, 70, 74, 75, 81, 88, 89, 108, 112, 115, 125, 127, 128, 133, 134, 153, 156, 158, 162, 164, 171; condition 35, 133; focus 36, 133, 168; interaction 37, 134, 168; time and space 34, 35, 133, 168
phrasal verbs 74, 79
pluripotential 15
potentiality continuum 85
pragmatics 123, 164
prepositions 3, 9, 18, 32, 33, 64, 65, 66, 67, 68, 69, 70, 74, 80, 81, 91, 119, 172
prescriptivism 52

procedural memory 17
prosodics 123
psychocultural variables 25

Ratey, John 17
reciprocals 148
recoordination 30

scaffold 6, 12, 28, 155
Searle, John 111
shudder 36, 91
Sino-Tibetan 10
sociocultural variables 24
Solis, Ramon 87
Spain 2, 12, 20, 46, 51, 67, 69, 79, 82, 83, 85, 87, 88, 132, 149, 158
specificity and importance 45, 49, 55, 56, 57, 58, 62, 162
subjunctivity 2, 3, 35, 46, 82, 83, 84, 85, 86, 87, 88, 89, 114, 121, 122, 165

tag questions 119
Tannen, Deborah 117
temporal expressions 139
Tevye 85, 86
the 51; *see also* definite article
thin slicing 7
transitive verbs 33
Turkey 39
Turner, Mark 32, 74

undergoer 127, 128, 164
Université d'Angers 70
University of Washington 18

verb 33, 36, 67, 74, 95, 104, 107, 108, 125, 149, 164, 165, 166
voice 35, 119, 121, 122, 124, 139, 157

Walmart 65, 66, 67, 157
Ward, Marrion 29
Wernicke's area 12
wh-questions 116, 117
Widdowson, Henry 8
Wilson, Bill 36, 37, 171
Wooten, Janice 54

yes/no questions 116, 117, 118

Zen 92, 96, 97, 155, 173
Zucker, Connie 7

www.ingramcontent.com/pod-product-compliance
Ingram Content Group UK Ltd.
Pitfield, Milton Keynes, MK11 3LW, UK
UKHW041919140426
5217IPUK00013B/231